SAMURAI SWORDSMANSHIP

THE BATTO, KENJUTSU AND TAMESHIGIRI OF EISHIN-RYU

MASAYUKI SHIMABUKURO
AND CARL E. LONG

BLACK BELT®
P R E S E N T S

SAMURAI SWORDSMANSHIP

THE BATTO, KENJUTSU AND TAMESHIGIRI OF EISHIN-RYU

MASAYUKI SHIMABUKURO
AND CARL E. LONG

Black Belt Books, Oklahoma City, OK 73110
Copyright © 2011 Cruz Bay Publishing, Inc
All Rights Reserved
Printed in China

Fifth Printing 2020

Library of Congress Number: 2011924529
ISBN-10: 0-89750-199-3
ISBN-13: 978-0-89750-199-6

Edited by Sarah Dzida
Cover and Graphic Design by John Bodine
Photography by Robert Reiff

For information about permission to reproduce selections from this book,
write Black Belt Books, 1000 Century Blvd., Oklahoma City OK 73110

BLACK BELT
P U B L I S H I N G
A Devision of **BLACK BELT**
MAGAZINE 1000

TABLE OF CONTENTS

ACKNOWLEDGMENTS

A book is unlike any other form of modern communication. It is personal and it is intimate. To bring a set of ideas, movement and passion to a blank page takes commitment, support, encouragement and inspiration from many individuals. In this book, we have set about to convey a message through the written word, reaching out through a medium that will hopefully add to the lives of others as much as it has enriched our own. We are sword practitioners and claim no particular aptitude for communicating through the written word, but with the help, talent and the encouragement of many individuals, this book, however humble, was made possible. We would like to acknowledge and thank certain people for their dedication and service in bringing knowledge, content, expertise and support to this project.

The content in the following chapters would not be possible if it were not for the generations of sword practitioners that sacrificed to maintain an unbroken chain of tradition. Our deep respect is offered to the late *sensei* Kono Hyakuren, who was the architect of *dai nihon batto-ho waza*. In addition, *hanshi* Miura Takeyuki has provided us with an inspirational model of how a person can exemplify samurai principles and ethics and make them relevant to a modern world. We wish to acknowledge the tireless service of the *hombu* directors of the Dai Nippon Butoku Kai for their work to preserve the classical and modern Japanese martial arts. Our humble gratitude is also offered to Dr. Hiroyuki Tesshin Hamada for his personal support and service to our efforts.

Our colleagues have improved this book far beyond what it might have been if left to our meager ability. Deserved recognition and appreciation goes to Chuck Arnold for illustrations, Michael Gunshannon for photography, Erik Johnstone for editorial support and to *Black Belt* for giving us access to resources and a talented and professional staff throughout this project. Perhaps the greatest contribution they provided was the aptitude and patience of our editor, Sarah Dzida, without whose expertise none of this would have been possible.

And finally, we wish to give heartfelt thanks and praise to our loving families who have sacrificed quality time with us so that projects such as these could be completed. Included in this family are the close friends and philanthropic partners who make it possible for us to continue our passion.

Thank you all.

—Masayuki Shimabukuro
Carl E. Long
2011

ABOUT THE AUTHORS

Masayuki Shimabukuro, Hanshi

Masayuki Shimabukuro was born in March 1948 in Osaka, Japan. Shimabukuro was an eighth *dan* in *Muso jikiden eishin-ryu iaijutsu,* an eighth dan in *Shito-ryu karatedo,* a seventh dan in *Shindo muso-ryu jojutsu* and received the title of *hanshi* (exemplary warrior) in both *karatedo* and *iaido.* He was the senior disciple of Miura Takeyuki Hidefusa. Shimabukuro held the position of chairman of the Jikishin-Kai International and the Kokusai Nippon Budo Kai. The Dai Nippon Butoku Kai recognized him as 21st soshihan in the lineage of the Masaoka line of *Eishin-ryu.* Shimabukuro also received official appointment by the Dai Nippon Butoku Kai as the school's international representative for iaido and *battodo* divisions.

In addition to being the *Black Belt* Hall of Fame 2006 Weapons Instructor of the Year, Shimabukuro wrote *Flashing Steel: Mastering Eishin-Ryu Swordsmanship* and *Katsu Jin Ken—Living Karate—The Way to Self Mastery* as well as the DVD series *Samurai Swordsmanship.* He passed away September 7, 2012. To learn more about Shimabukuro, please visit jikishin-kai.com.

Carl E. Long, Kyoshi

Carl Long teaches and resides in Kingston, Pennsylvania. He began his martial arts studies in 1968. He is the vice chairman and director for the Jikishin-Kai International and is responsible for the instruction and certification of Jikishin-Kai and Kokusai Nippon Budo Kai instructors in North America, South America and Europe. He has achieved advanced master level ranks in Muso jikiden eishin-ryu iaijutsu, Shindo muso-ryu jojutsu, *Shorin-ryu karate, Shito-ryu karate* and *Okinawa kobudo.* He has earned the title of *kyoshi* from the Kokusai Nippon Budo Kai and the Dai Nippon Butoku Kai. Long is a five-time recipient of the Dai Nippon Butoku Kai's prestigious *yushu-sho,* which is the highest award granted for the performance of iaido in Asia, North America and Europe. In 2008, he was appointed as an official representative and coordinator for the Dai Nippon Budo Kai iaido division. Long wrote articles for the column Cutting Edge in *Black Belt* for several years. To learn more about Long, visit sakurabudokan.com.

PREFACE

Throughout the ages, man's achievements and failures have been framed by this one single inquiry: Why are we here? The search for an answer has become the "Great Conversation" that has taken place between men of great intellect over time. Every society and culture that has existed has posed the question and attempted to find the answer through some form of exploration—science, arts or religions—in order to move closer to enlightenment. Eastern approaches have taken a holistic approach to solving the riddle, whereas Western approaches have dissected methods of research and exploration into categories that concentrate on a single aspect of the physical, mental and spiritual in order to get at the facts. In the end, the answer to "why are we here" still seems to be elusive.

In a modern world with so much available at a person's fingertips, it's easy to ignore the "Great Conversation." It's much easier to believe in the delusion that the struggles of one person or country are not shared by others—that pain and suffering is somehow unique only to the individual or a certain segment of the population. It's as if a person chooses to view his place in the world within the reach of his hand rather than as part of a larger organism that functions only when the health of the entire system is good.

For the men and women born to samurai families of ancient Japan, they understood their purpose as it was part of that larger organism, and it was simple—to serve others. The reality that they might have to give their life in the service of their *daimyo* or country at any moment was constantly in the forefront of their consciousness. To a samurai, the last day could always be the present one. How they chose to live became the quintessence of their existence. The things that mattered most to them were those things that would benefit society as a whole, such as acts of loyalty, courtesy, sincerity, compassion, courage, justice and honor. For the samurai, these acts were the things that defined him and answered the question, "Why are we here?"

It is the authors' opinion that the ethical and moral tenets that the samurai lived by are characteristics that are beneficial to all societies. Hundreds of years have been invested in developing this system of service and behavior that takes into account the welfare and protection of others. Even though the methods associated with Japanese swordsmanship may be an antiquated means of waging war in this modern age, they offer a suitable way to live life in peace.

The techniques, philosophy and history presented in this book are meant to impart a better understanding of the essence of samurai swordsmanship. Our mission in presenting the material is to ensure that those who are interested in replicating the footsteps of the old masters of the art will have a deeper understanding of the nature of their journey. It is also our hope that the practices and messages associated with the *kenjutsu, battojutsu* and *tameshigiri* presented in this manual will help to strengthen the mind, body and spirit of our readers. But even more, it is our mission to see that these practices benefit the families and communities of the practitioner through the evolution of his character.

We have chosen to present the standing methods of the *Eishin-ryu batto-ho* as a standard for readers to practice and explore. The term battojutsu as opposed to *iaijutsu* is used throughout the book to denote the Japanese method of sword drawing. However, the two terms are often used interchangeably in modern sword practice. These technical sets of *waza* were created for the Japan-based organization Dai Nippon Butoku Kai by the students of Oe Masamichi, who was the last samurai headmaster of the

Eishin-ryu tradition. As members and representatives of the Dai Nippon Butoku Kai, the authors feel a sense of responsibility to our seniors in the art of Eishin-ryu and to the founders of the modern method of transmitting this Japanese art form. The health and welfare of the Western sword practitioner was the inspiration for presenting the reader with these standing techniques. Here in the West, most people are unaccustomed to sitting in traditional postures on the floor. It is also difficult for those with injuries or infirmities to assume these positions. Thus, people of all ages and physical conditions will be able to comfortably practice the Eishin-ryu standing techniques. Readers will also see that practicing Japanese swordsmanship from a standing posture is no less desirable than beginning from a seated posture if they read the historical timeline of Eishin-ryu kenjutsu that is available in the appendix section of the book.

Once the reader assimilates all the information in this book, we promote the study and practice of all other traditional sets of waza. Fortunately, battojutsu has become readily available to the Western world in the past fifty years. The availability of qualified instructors offers many opportunities for those wishing to seek further information. We encourage you to explore the techniques and concepts, history and philosophy presented in this book and then seek guidance and instruction from a qualified teacher.

—Masayuki Shimabukuro
Carl E. Long
2011

CHAPTER 1

PHILOSOPHY OF
JAPANESE SWORDSMANSHIP

Sword-drawing technique or *battojutsu* is a unique practice that is different from *kenjutsu*. Of course, many kenjutsu styles include *batto* as a component of their training, but there is a difference between styles designated as kenjutsu and styles classified distinctly as battojutsu. Kenjutsu refers to sword methods that take place once the sword has already been drawn. Battojutsu also addresses a scenario of face-to-face combat but it is a response to an attack or combative situation while the sword is still in the scabbard. Battojutsu imparts methods of instantaneously defending against an attack, often from a disadvantageous position, which means the practitioner must draw his sword and cut simultaneously. Kenjutsu refers to everything that happens after the draw has been completed.

There are obviously many *waza* in battojutsu. The waza recreate possible combative scenarios, but it is a mistake to think of a waza as a single method of dealing with a specific attack. Instead, you should think of the curriculum of waza as an alphabet in that each technique represents a letter. However, just knowing the alphabet is not enough. You must understand how each letter can be combined with other letters to form words.

Waza works this way, as well. Each technique imparts principles and methods of properly using the sword, and like the letters of the alphabet, they can stand alone or in combination to express an idea. Eventually, the various techniques and principles of one waza can be combined with methods from other waza, resulting in *kae waza,* variations that express an alternative strategy or concept. In fact, the combining of waza into formal techniques is seen in many other kenjutsu styles, too.

When you understand the waza of the curriculum of a given *ryu*, you'll see that a single waza actually contains many possibilities—one sword can become 10,000 swords, and one waza can become 10,000 waza. This concept is perhaps best represented in the classical kenjutsu style of *Ono-ha itto-ryu.* In this style of kenjutsu, the application of *kirioroshi* is the most important technique learned in the first *kumitachi* (paired drill). This first waza is the most important of all the kumitachi because everything in the ryu is built off of it and always returns to it. This is in fact, the very meaning of *"itto,"* which means one sword.

This same idea is found in all kenjutsu styles, like in *nukitsuke* of *Eishin-ryu batto-ho,* which is the technical focus of this book. You'll see how everything in the book begins with and comes back to nukitsuke.

But, from the standpoint of self-defense, what is the value of understanding battojutsu in the modern age? The sword is an archaic weapon, but battojutsu actually contains principles that are applicable to the root of many empty-hand *jujutsu*-related arts. An expression of this idea is found within the practice of *muto-dori,* which refers to unarmed methods of defense against an opponent wielding a sword. In short, you take the sword from the attacker. (This is why Japanese swordsmanship can also be applied to auxiliary weapons, such as the *tessen.*) Practitioners with a high level of battojutsu skill and understanding will probably even be able to create empty-hand techniques directly from the study of battojutsu, but it will be the result of many years of dedicated practice.

THE DEFINING ELEMENTS OF BATTOJUTSU

The basic components of Eishin-ryu battojutsu can be distilled down to four primary techniques. These essential components are the first draw, the finishing cut, the ceremonial cleaning of the blade and the return of the blade to its scabbard. Although they may seem to be independent of one another, they are all considered a continuation of the very first movement, which is known as nukitsuke.

NUKITSUKE

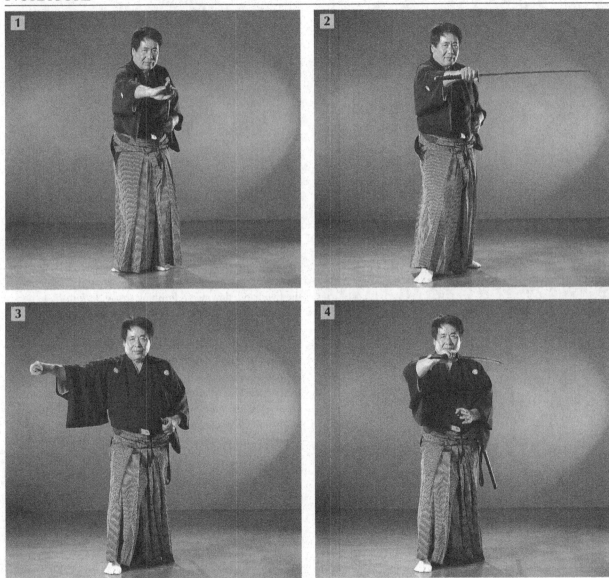

1-4: When performing *nukitsuke*, the drawing action begins slowly as if to allow the opponent the time to reconsider the outcome of his actions. Therefore, nukitsuke becomes a life-giving technique. The practitioner does not focus on winning but rather on stopping his opponent's aggressive behavior and preserving life. In the last moment of nukitsuke, known as *saya banare*, the sword leaves the scabbard. This action appears to happen seemingly on its own accord to cut down evil intentions and therefore restore order. Immediately following the initial drawing action, the practitioner moves to raise the sword above his head to perform a downward two-hand cut.

KIRIOROSHI

1-3: Throughout the history of *Eishin-ryu*, the master's responsibility has always been to give life to the traditions and spirit of the founder while at the same time adapting the art's relevance to the modern world. A critical wound on the ancient battlefield meant untold suffering. The samurai considered the two-hand, downward finishing stroke, *kirioroshi*, to be the humane way to end the suffering of a mortally wounded enemy. Kirioroshi should remind a practitioner that ethical and morally-just actions should be an aid to ending the suffering of others. It is through the act of kirioroshi that a swordsman can end suffering through his practice of samurai swordsmanship. True understanding of compassion through the sincere intention to end the suffering of others leads the swordsman to make positive contributions to society. Through kirioroshi, the practitioner seeks to attain both social and self-perfection.

CHIBURI

1: There are many methods of ceremoniously cleaning the blade, and each *waza* ends with a procedure for acting out the cleaning process. These methods would be done quickly on the battlefield before resheathing the sword. Later a full cleaning of the blade would be required after the imminent danger of combat had passed. This ritual act of cleansing the sword is known as *chiburi*. Within the art of *battojutsu*, there are several methods of cleaning the blade. Each method utilizes a particular series of movements to symbolically as well as practically remove the gore from the sword. The blade is also thought to mirror the intentions of the warrior. It is for this reason that the *katana* is often referred to as "the soul of the samurai." For if the swordsman has performed *nukitsuke* to preserve life and *kirioroshi* as an act to end the suffering of another, then his conscience and soul are free from the negative aspects of violence for violence's sake. Therefore, the actual physical cleaning of the blade is always done with the proper equipment.

NOTO

1: In each *waza*, the swordsman must return the sword to the *saya* (scabbard). The act of resheathing the sword is known as *noto*. Noto gives the swordsman the opportunity to practice lingering awareness because he must return the sword in an efficient manner without exposing himself to attack. This action is performed with the feeling of completing the waza and maintaining the awareness that there may still be evil in the minds of others. Resolving the past and being ever mindful of the present, the practitioner generates the realization that he must be ever diligent to control his mind and not allow it to become complacent or lulled into an undue sense of security.

Because nukitsuke endows the swordsman with insight that lives hang in the balance of this very first drawing cut, nukitsuke is often referred to as the "life of *iai*." Unlike empty-hand techniques, a sword cut will always leave an indelible mark in the world. Once the sword has left the *saya* (scabbard), it will change a life forever because it is meant to strike down the enemy before he can attack or retreat. The separation of the sword from the saya is intentionally meant to separate the life force of your opponent from his body. You can easily draw parallels to how the sheathed sword represents the stable and balanced forces of nature whereas the lethal cut of the sword separates the manifest and non-manifest union of what is recognized as a human's existence. Battojutsu changes the life of your opponent, his family, community and everyone whose life he may have touched in even some small way, forever. Likewise the victor in this encounter will change forever as well. Therefore, the trained practitioner strives to confirm that all life is precious and that the taking of such is not without consequences. After all, if a person is the sum of all his experiences, then he will eventually become a result of his actions and experiences.

Today, practice should promote the notion of a life-giving sword *(katsu jin ken)*. Your practice is meant to preserve the life of the swordsman and not to take the life of your enemy *(satsu jin to)*. Although this may seem like an argument of semantics, it is actually predicated on what the swordsman's intention is that gives life to his technique. Nukitsuke with a sword in your hand is much like the words that come forth from your mouth. Think of how people are sometimes accused of having a sharp tongue. Once the words have left your lips, they can never be retrieved. No apology can take back the suffering of those that have been hurt by harmful statements. Impetuous actions lead to regret and are the result of a lack of self-control. Through these four seemingly simple acts—nukitsuke, *kirioroshi, chiburi, noto*—the modern swordsman develops *heijoshin,* which is a calm and peaceful spirit that is unaffected by the daily ups and downs that modern living presents. He may not need to carry a sword in modern society, but the need to develop a razor sharp mind and a clear, focused spirit is as much a part of battojutsu today as it was centuries ago.

SAYA NO NAKA NO KATCHI

The spirit and intention of the ancient and modern samurai is focused on achieving his highest goal: attaining victory without drawing, cutting or killing an enemy. He wants to win without violence or confrontation. This philosophy is encapsulated in the phrase *"saya no naka no katchi,"* which means "victory while the sword is still in the scabbard." Of course, this is a noble view of *budo* ethics, but how does the practitioner accomplish it in his everyday interactions?

There are essentially two ways to do it. First, the practitioner can train diligently to become a highly skilled swordsman who is physically strong and technically able. To illustrate this way, it's best to turn to the example of the legendary Japanese swordsman Miyamoto Musashi. Once, Musashi and his disciple Jotaro were walking beneath a boulder that was precariously perched on the edge of a cliff. Jotaro was afraid to walk under it because he believed the rock would crush them. Musashi responded, *"Iwao wo mi."* What this means is that the key to victory for a warrior is to be like the boulder on the cliff: immovable and containing great hidden power. It causes fear in anyone who comes near it.

Musashi believed that this was the highest expression of training. However, it's important to remember that "iwao no mi" can lead to an overly aggressive mindset when not tempered with compassion, which leads to a worldview that is rooted in violence. An old teaching says, "Through your thoughts, you create your world." Therefore, if you see someone or think of someone as an enemy, you are certain to cause them to become one. And if you see enemies everywhere, your life will be filled with conflict. Conversely, if you treat everyone well, you can create conditions that allow for a very peaceful mind.

A legend surrounding Musashi and the Zen monk Takuan Soho once again serves as a model for these ideas. In this story, a venomous snake crept toward Takuan while he and Musashi were sitting *zazen* beside a stream. As the snake moved up to Takuan and slithered harmlessly over his lap, the motionless monk merely smiled. On reaching Musashi, however, the snake recoiled in fear and slithered into the brush. While Musashi had not moved, his fierce spirit was palpable to the snake, causing it to flee to the safety of the brush. At the same time, Musashi became aware of the difference in spirit between him and Takuan. He realized that in training for so long to cultivate such strong technique and spirit, no one would ever dare attack him. The great sword master could defeat an opponent without striking a blow, but he was also a man that no one could ever be close to. In Takuan, Musashi observed the result of equally arduous training, but his training manifested as a quiet, calm strength and great peace. Takuan's spirit of naturalness had a far greater power to affect others in a positive way than Musashi's fierce spirit ever could.

This story provides keys concerning the second way that modern practitioners can train to manifest the concept of "saya no naka no katchi." "Iwao no mi" equally provides fertile soil from which a truly authentic heijoshin can grow. You can most certainly train for strong martial technique, but you must also train with the proper heart and spirit. This is what will lead to true strength of spirit, which will in turn manifest as an authentic peaceful mind.

Of course, pacifism without strength is often a recipe for exploitation or domination. An old samurai maxim states, "Only a warrior can choose pacifism; all others are condemned to it." Unfortunately, modern budo is often practiced in a very passive manner, and battojutsu is a common example of this. Too often, battojutsu is reduced to a mere sword-drawing practice for "spiritual" development or "aesthetic" appreciation. It is often performed with no *kihaku* (martial content). The reality is that focusing on "pretty" battojutsu develops nothing. In the end, practitioners should seek the strength and confidence of "iwao no mi" tempered by compassion and wisdom in their battojutsu training.

CULTIVATING SOFT POWER

The role of the samurai was to protect his country, society and family. This is the true ideal of the samurai and is as important in modern times as it was in feudal Japan. Today, many people practice various forms of martial arts, including those with roots in the samurai tradition. Yet how many of them actually live according to the ideals of the samurai? How many are developing *budo no seishin* (warrior's spirit)?

Many people live lives of apathy, and that is not an example of *budo no seishin*. Instead practitioners must live and act positively, proactively and with compassion. The practice of martial arts only for exercise, sport, self-defense or even self-improvement is limiting and, perhaps, even selfish. Instead, those who study budo must do so with others in mind. All martial artists have to have a responsibility and obligation to their society and their country. As such, practitioners of samurai swordsmanship must do what they can to help others and they must strive, through their actions, to build a better society.

Through budo training, students develop physical power, but they also must develop "soft power" so that they can become well-equipped to make sound decisions. As a result, *budoka* help to reshape society exponentially, and at the same time, truly begin to achieve victory while the sword is in the saya.

CHAPTER 2

THE PATH TO
JAPANESE SWORDSMANSHIP

A swordsman can choose to never look at his swordsmanship as anything more than technical skills to be mastered for combat or sport. It is entirely up to him whether or not to question his motivations or to examine the ethical or moral implications of when and why the sword is drawn. Practicing *bujutsu* as a budo is a choice. But it is not independent of bujutsu. It is not automatic. However, in the 19th and 20th centuries, the pursuit of self-actualization became the focal point of many styles of kenjutsu. The elemental techniques of the sword arts fulfilled a philosophical role in the moral education of the samurai, and they continue to satisfy that role for many practitioners who still keep these methods alive today.

THE ROAD TO SELF-ACTUALIZATION—WAZA, JUTSU, DO

The learning curve for the beginner is always the steepest. In most cases everything that is presented to him is new. The environment often seems foreign and the customs totally unfamiliar. By the time the student of budo is taught the first fundamental sword technique, he has most likely already been exposed to multiple new relationships and *dojo* customs. Each step is another rung on a vertical ladder. The task of taking a step upward is a trial in itself.

Waza represents the building blocks of the art because without waza there can be no art. All sword arts begin with the student first learning the fundamentals of the craft, and the fundamentals at this stage are the most basic elements of posture, grip, swing, etc. These basic techniques must become comfortable to the student before they can be done in combination. As the fundamentals are built on, other techniques are introduced, and the student's repertoire of movements increases. More combinations of techniques are assembled and the student develops a sense of the curriculum that he is expected to be responsible for. In this waza stage of training, technique is all that exists for the trainee. This is the stage wherein the practitioner is physically and mentally attached to the technical aspects of performing the movement. The task of remembering, coordinating and assembling the individual components that have been learned still occupy the largest portion of the student's training time.

The next period of development is the *jutsu* stage. This period of development is not as easy to recognize as the waza stage. The jutsu stage begins to expose itself naturally over a period of years. For the student, some techniques still require thought while others seem to be naturally evolving into reflexive and conditioned responses. The waza has begun to come to life. The movements begin to acquire purpose each time the practitioner performs them. He has a sense of timing and distance that is required to make the technique work. The technician and the technique begin to reflect each other. The technician can adapt to the changing circumstances and the technique is understood to be flexible and representative of all other techniques in the swordsman's arsenal. If he were a painter, he would be able to duplicate a landscape or human form so that others would recognize the depiction. His ability to capture the nuance of the scene would be instantly recognizable to the observer. The artist in this phase of his development chooses the correct paints in combinations that would have seemed totally foreign to him in the waza stage of development. However, the student is frustrated by the flaws he sees in everything he achieves. He now understands what a daunting task it will be for him to become natural and accomplished at all of the waza. The training process becomes a huge circle that returns back on itself. Every technique that becomes natural opens a door to a new technique that is once again practiced as waza before it can be totally claimed by the swordsman. During this stage, the student may even be referred to as a master swordsman, but to him, there will always be innumerable unanswered questions that need to be researched and explored. The thought of mastery becomes elusive and practice itself is now the primary motivation for training. It will take many years to arrive at the level of jutsu. There are no shortcuts or secrets to getting there. Time, sweat, patience and the desire to improve are the only ingredients for success.

Eventually during training, the swordsman will experience a *kensho* (a window) to his subconscious mind that opens up to the true nature of his desire to train. He will begin to question and examine his motivations and purpose. At this point in the swordsman's evolution, the integrated waza continues to develop, but his practice now becomes a thermometer and a barometer by which he can measure the temperature and pressure in his life. Each cutting technique uniquely reflects the temperament and intention of the swordsman. It is recognizable to him as an indicator of his present nature and his reaction and response to his own environment. Practice for the student at this complex *"do"* stage is not independent of waza or jutsu. Waza and jutsu are necessary for his practice to even be possible. To practice a martial art at the "do" stage, as a road to self-actualization, the practitioner must channel the technical aspects of swordsmanship so they reflect and reveal his depth of character.

These stages of development should not be confused with the principles and concepts of *shu, ha* and *ri*—the copy, divergence and transcending of technique. Instead, waza, jutsu and "do" are stages of development that the practitioner passes through as his understanding and skills evolve. Also, he can choose to stay at any of the levels leading up to the "do" stage.

THE MORAL TRAINING OF A SWORDSMAN

Whatever the reasons that people begin their study of martial arts, it is very common for many practitioners to focus their practice solely on the polishing of technique. This attention to the execution of waza is initially as common in the sword arts as it is in other martial arts. While the development of correct technique is of vital importance to understanding the deeper principles and philosophy of the classical sword arts, merely focusing on technique is not enough to realize the value of the traditional martial arts in everyday life.

The goal of training that is traditionally pursued through the practice of swordsmanship is the understanding and implementation of *bushido* and its value to communities and culture. Bushido, which is often translated as the "way of the warrior," is the samurai "code of ethics" that developed during feudal Japan and was formalized during the Tokugawa Shogunate.

As a natural outgrowth of the values of the samurai class and its rules of conduct in daily life, bushido, along with the samurai class itself, has come to symbolize the Japanese martial arts. Bushido is characterized by the following seven virtues: righteousness, courage, compassion, respect, honor, sincerity and loyalty. Although bushido may seem to be merely an antiquated code of conduct developed by a warrior class of Japan's feudal past, it is widely believed that the teachings of bushido have profound relevance in modern society. As a tangible code of ethics that is based on fairness, politeness, and self-control, bushido, as studied through etiquette and conduct of traditional budo (martial ways), serves as *dotoku kyoiku* (moral education) of proper conduct in daily life.

A practitioner's training in budo may serve to provide this moral education by teaching characteristics that are of utmost importance, including courtesy, honor, duty and the determination to honor an obligation regardless of the circumstances. Additionally, the moral education that is offered through training may allow a practitioner to reach a very high goal, such as victory over one's self or self-mastery. While the goal of self-mastery is certainly of great personal benefit, the higher purpose of self-mastery is to benefit others. Like the samurai before him, a practitioner should strive to apply the moral education that he has learned through the teachings of bushido as a way to self-mastery in order to have the greatest positive effect in any situation that he may encounter. It is also important to understand that while practitioners seek victory over themselves, they are not seeking victory over others. Rather, their attitude with respect to relationships and interactions with others is "not to lose." This principle of "not losing" is applied to yourself as well as to others with whom you may interact. These are the principles that make bushido very different from sports, in which the objective of any game or contest is to win.

Sadly, the dotoku that bushido provides seems to be missing in much of society. What is frequently observed and often considered to be proper conduct is actually completely devoid of any real heart or higher purpose. This artifice does nothing to replace the "me first" attitude in society with that of self-mastery for the benefit of others. The absence of this moral education in many segments of society is thus expressed in unfair, cowardly conduct and, most alarmingly, violence against others. This was the most shameful condition for samurai, and by extension, is just as shameful for budoka of today.

At the same time, the dotoku of bushido can still be found in many dojo today. Indeed, it is the responsibility of any good dojo to provide a model education because society is clearly in need of these teachings. Good budo is so much more than simply swinging a sword well or executing a powerful strike or throw. Budo is the embodiment of the positive characteristics of bushido.

In fact, without the moral education that bushido provides, budo would be little more than the study of systemized violence. Bushido, which evolved as a model of conduct for the samurai class, is as relevant in today's society as it was in feudal Japan. Bushido and the moral education that it provides continues to teach the positive qualities that serve as the glue that binds Japanese society today. It is this moral education of bushido—that provides a foundation of proper courtesy and a positive, selfless philosophy—that tempers the potential to cause harm. It transforms martial arts into pathways that provide the tools to build better communities and a better society.

THE SEVEN VIRTUES OF BUSHIDO

GI Righteousness and Rectitude	*Bushido* is based on doing what is right for the sake of others. It was the duty of each samurai to protect and serve his family, community and nation. The individual goals of the samurai were expected to be ignored if they were in conflict with doing what was right for others. Therefore, *gi* (righteousness and rectitude) is the decision to choose a course of action based on the rational and conventional knowledge of what is right and wrong. A person's own self-centered ambitions tempt him to act selfishly. These selfish feelings can sway him away from doing the right things, and even kindness can lead him away from doing what he knows to be correct. Gi is the cornerstone to all of the other virtues of bushido.
REI Courtesy and Etiquette	Society has given people ethical and moral standards for the purpose of easing the friction between men. Therefore, *rei* is the sincere respect that each person should hold for those around him. This respect must be sincere and not an affectation. Courtesy and etiquette permeate the day-to-day interactions between most people. Rei may at times be thought of as the act of expressing respect for others by bowing. But it is the term *o-jiki* that refers to the actual act of the bow. The act of o-jiki on the outside can be no more than the respect you feel for others on the inside.
JIN Compassion	*Jin* may be thought of as "benevolence" or "compassion" for others. Compassion was believed to be the character of a true and just leader. The benevolent leader had the respect of those he led. Samurai were at the top of the ruling class. They controlled the ultimate fate of those who lived to support them, and yet they understood that power must be tempered with respect and compassion for those who were there to support their needs. Many took up the study of painting and calligraphy while others learned arts to develop a sense of beauty in all things. For it was believed that without the ability to see beauty in simplicity, a man would not be capable of benevolence or compassion.
YU Courage	A true samurai did not fear death. That does not mean that he sought death over life. He did not die flippantly or throw his life away haphazardly to demonstrate his courage because samurai were expected to protect others even if it meant sacrificing themselves. True courage comes from the knowledge that the cause is just and that it is greater than the individual needs of one person. Courage is the byproduct of righteousness. However, courage does not come without fear. It is moving forward in spite of fear for the sake of *gi* and *jin* (righteousness and compassion).

HOMARE Honor	The samurai concept of "honor" is perhaps the most difficult to describe. *Homare* or *meiyo* has more to do with a person's "good name." A man without honor does not suffer shame and loss of face. A samurai would go to great lengths to avoid losing his honor. His honor went far beyond his doorstep. It extended to his family, community and his feudal lord. It was considered unacceptable to do anything "un-samurai-like" that would weaken the reputation of not only his clan but his class of warriors. The thought of bringing shame upon his family or community was considered unforgivable. *Seppuku* (or ritual suicide) was a better alternative than leaving his family with the shame of losing their honor.
MAKOTO Sincerity	Words to a samurai meant that there was a promise being made to act in accordance with one's speech. If he were to declare his loyalty to a superior, it meant his actions would exemplify his words. Likewise, if he were to express sympathy for someone's condition, it meant his actions would demonstrate a true understanding of that person's condition. Sincerity is the cornerstone of *bushido*. Without sincerity, *makoto* or *shisei*, all of the other virtues are empty vessels.
CHU Duty and Loyalty	Duty and loyalty could not be separated in the mind of the samurai class. Their loyalty was given because they had the duty to serve. They were born into a class of society whose principle role was to serve as leaders and protectors. These duties extended from the lowest ranks of the samurai to the *shogun* himself. All were bound to do what was right for their lord and their loyalty was the sincere display of their commitment to their station in life. The loyalty to do what was righteous and just, courageous and benevolent for the sake of one's leader and country is the loyalty that was owed for having been born samurai.

THE TEACHER-STUDENT RELATIONSHIP

Shi is teacher. *Tei* is student. *Ai* is love or harmony. *Shi tei ai* refers to the master/disciple or teacher/student relationship and indicates a strong connection based on compassion, respect, obligation and responsibility. The importance of the teacher/student relationship cannot be overstated and is absolutely essential in your growth as a sword practitioner.

The path to learning any martial art initially begins the same: by finding a mentor you trust to teach you the skills that are necessary for success. The Japanese word *sensei* translates as "one who has gone before." Therefore, your sensei should be a normal person with a desire to share his knowledge and experience with others. His demeanor and skills should inspire others to achieve their greatest potential. It is impossible to learn from someone who you feel does not have your best interests at heart. In addition, the skills and experience of this teacher determine the speed and depth of which the information is disseminated.

Choosing a teacher is a conscious decision. Finding a teacher that you trust with your life, literally when swinging a sword, should not be taken lightly. Don't look for someone to be your friend. The teacher-student relationship should be different than all of the other relationships in your life. It is unique. But what do you look for? Should you primarily look for superior technical skill? Perhaps his rank or title is the most important. As a beginner, how would you know?

All of these things give some indication of a teacher's experience but they do not convey the essential qualities of a teacher of budo. A good budo teacher should have *jinkaku;* this term refers to an outgoing personality. This is a necessity and, in many cases, is of greater importance than a sensei's rank because jinkaku refers to a person's ability to see and understand himself objectively. This is an essential quality for instructors because of the *seikinin* (personal responsibility) for the direction and growth of their students. An instructor will have a profound influence or impact in the lives of his students. As such, the personal qualities and habits of a teacher, positive or negative, can "transfer" to his students, very possibly affecting their future. An instructor must therefore have a clear view and understanding of his habits, thoughts, actions and self-expression. There are many students who, having been strongly influenced by their teachers, become teachers themselves and act exactly like their teachers. Remember that a student becomes a reflection of the teacher, exhibiting many of that teacher's qualities, good or bad. That's why a person with a good, likeable and compassionate personality is much more likely to attract and maintain students than a person who lacks such qualities. An instructor with jinkaku will be much more effective in helping others improve themselves in life.

Good budo teachers also guide the development of a student's strength and attitude. *Seishin* is correct attitude and, in this case, it refers to the attitude with which a person should approach the meaning and execution of his or her technique. In feudal Japan, the role of a sensei was clear: to effectively transmit the methods that would enable a swordsman to be effective in face-to-face combat. As such, both teacher and student could realize their roles in the protection of life, society and country. The purpose for study in our time is different from that of feudal Japan, but instructors must still understand and manifest seishin. The spirit of the protection of life, society and country must be in any practitioner's heart. This requires an understanding of *toho,* which is the proper meaning in the use of the sword. Waza must therefore be faithfully executed in accordance with the methods handed down to an instructor from preceding generations of teachers. The instructor's *gijutsu,* as reflected in his execution of waza, should be polished or "high-level" technique and not limited to mere aesthetic qualities. A good instructor will constantly train, understand and demonstrate both waza and jutsu in order to improve as a technician. He always keeps his mind on *kenkyu,* which is a thorough research of the methods of the ryu. In fact, if the teacher has been training for many years, he will exhibit passion and knowledge of *michi*—this is another pronunciation of "do" (the way). Here, michi refers to a commitment to spread budo from person to person (expressed by the principle of *fukyu)* to benefit people and society as a whole.

A skilled teacher guides the members of the dojo toward their highest life condition. The teacher creates the atmosphere by example and leads by his demonstration of courtesy and etiquette. Etiquette is difficult to teach to those who are not familiar with bushido. It requires correction and critique, but as the budoka achieves greater knowledge, skill and understanding of battojutsu, his head will bow lower to the mat because of the weight and responsibility he now carries.

Of course, the teacher is only one variable in the equation for success. A credible teacher will set the tone and establish the path for others to follow but he does not walk this path for the students. The attitude and the determination of each student in the dojo contribute to the overall atmosphere that permeates the training hall. Successful trainees have similar qualities that can be viewed as the traits that set them apart from those who are less serious about their art.

The time spent in the dojo is time taken away from family, friends and other pursuits. However, those who pursue budo eventually understand that they have already invested the most valuable thing they have in their training—their time. A keen student understands that monetary investments in his training are inconsequential compared to the investment of time that he has already chosen to make. These people do not hesitate to invest in the appropriate equipment that is necessary for their training. They acquire the best for what they can afford rather than spend frivolously on other things that do not enhance their lives.

In every dojo, there are those students that everyone wishes to train with. They are the first people that are asked to be a partner during kumitachi and are the same people whose company others enjoy after class. It is easy to pick these students out from the rest. They are the ones with a bright and positive attitude. They create a positive environment for those around them. These are the people that seem to keep negativity out of their lives. That does not mean that they live in a world without fears or suffering. They choose to see obstacles as signs that they are moving forward. For these individuals, each obstacle represents a mile marker ensuring them that they are always making progress. Not surprisingly, these same students always seem to have high optimism. Their expectations of themselves and others are great. Even when corrected or while receiving a harsh critique from their teacher, they exhibit gratitude and respect for the opportunity to grow and improve. These are the students that make overwhelming progress. It is this group that forms the core of seniors in a dojo and inspires others to succeed. Their encouragement and demeanor is supportive and humble.

A practitioner that wishes to learn Japanese budo, particularly the sword arts should attempt to emulate the qualities that others find beneficial to the society. These qualities will serve them well within the dojo to support the training of others and outside of the dojo to achieve their goals and aspirations.

The relationship between the teacher and the student extends far beyond what can be seen. The *on-giri* (obligation and duty) of both teacher and student extend to a relationship that both have with the ryu. The tradition that they attempt to maintain and breathe life into has been bequeathed to them through a succession of budoka, many of whom made the ultimate sacrifice for the protection, preservation and evolution of the art they study. Unlike in the modern era where warfare is waged with sterile technologies, the samurai engaged in combat that was intimate. The swordsman was present to see the light leave the eyes of his enemy. It was under these conditions that the principles and practices we study today are based. The methods that survived were passed along by the men who stayed alive by using them. However, that laboratory is no longer available nor do modern practitioners wish to return to it. Instead, samurai members of the ryu synthesized and distilled a legacy of sword methods of which we are now the stewards.

This book is written during the fifth century of the tradition of Japanese sword methods. The sword school of Eishin-ryu dates back to Hayashizaki Jinsuke and can be traced through the footsteps of 20 or more generations across time. Each member of a legitimate Japanese sword art is capable of tracing the heritage of their ryu backward in time through a succession of student-teacher relationships than span centuries if not millennia. But it only exists today because of the teacher you are learning it from. It only exists tomorrow should you decide to practice and preserve it. These ancient sword arts are extant only if there is someone who is committed to their preservation and performance. The next generation's inheritance rests solely with the dedication and stewardship of those who breathe life into the tradition today. Sword technique must be performed to be of any substance. These *koryu* arts are not things that existed in the past and are relics that are dug up in an archeological study. They are a living breathing entity that are kept alive by people who believe that there are benefits inherent in the practice of methods created many years ago.

The challenge and obligation for both teachers and students is in maintaining the authenticity of the techniques that have been preserved. It is easy to cite examples of commercialism and distortion of the original methods and intent. Because whenever a teacher or practitioner of the art loses sight of his duty as a steward, he is tempted to modify the tradition for his own benefit. This rarely occurs when faced with the responsibility and knowledge that the art is not actually his property. It is in his possession for the short period of time he is able to continue to practice and then it is gone. It is gone! It is gone unless he decides to pass it on unaltered to the next generation of sincere students. This is the relationship that every practitioner, teacher or student has with the ryu. It is a relationship that stems from the respect for others' sacrifices and their role in the continuation of the ryu. The respect is fostered in the long hours of refining and correcting techniques and attitudes that are shared by teacher and student. Each develops a regard for the art that transcends their self-importance. They cultivate an atmosphere in the dojo and subsequently within the ryu that their practice is for *kodomo no tame ni*—the sake of the children—the next generation.

CHAPTER 3

THE FIRST
STEPS TO TRAINING

*S*aho means preparation. The efforts to prepare the dojo, training equipment and proper attire are not just for learning how to swing a sword in battle. They are preparation for the mind as well. Very few individuals today will ever find the need to use their swordsmanship skills to do battle against an armed opponent, but for the samurai, this was a daily realism. Because he could be called to action at a moment's notice, preparation for that life-or-death moment was completed with the utmost sincerity and diligence. Every possibility was considered. The contingencies of battle and the conditions under which they might take place were taken into account. Moreover, the possibility of it being a samurai's last day meant that preparations for death were as important as concerns about victory. The samurai's mission was to do his duty with honor and dignity, even if it was accompanied by death. A samurai put great emphasis on *midashi nami*—the appearance of things and how he represented his family, community and country in the eyes of others. Even in battle, his preparation included the burning of incense in the *kabuto* (helmet) so as not to offend the enemy should his head be presented as evidence of his demise. The attention to small details, such as where to stand in the dojo or which direction to turn, was an exercise in teaching a samurai how to move during battle. It strengthened the mind and prepared him to act through conditioned response.

Preparation exemplifies commitment and sincerity. The care and attention given to the dojo, training equipment and *keiko-gi* are a reflection of the sincerity of the budoka. A wrinkled *hakama* or dirty keiko-gi is the manifestation of an undisciplined mind.

THE UNIFORM

The sword cannot be properly manipulated from a drawing position unless the training uniform is worn correctly. The keiko-gi (uniform) is comprised of a cotton kimono-like jacket, a long cloth belt and the wide-legged hakama. Each part of the training uniform must be correctly positioned to facilitate freedom of movement as well as offer support for the sword as it is worn thrust through the belt and hakama. The *uwagi* (jacket) is worn like the standard uniform top found in most other Japanese martial arts except that it is longer and extends to the knees. Senior grades may elect to wear the traditional *montsuki* (formal kimono top), hakama and *tabi* (socks)

The *obi* (belt or sash) serves multiple purposes when worn under the hakama during battojutsu or kenjutsu practice. It holds the keiko-gi closed, anchors the hakama and supports the long and short swords. The support that a well-manufactured *kaku-obi* (square sash) gives to a heavy sword cannot be underestimated. A well-tied obi also prevents unnecessary movements when performing *taito, datto,* nukitsuke and noto. There are several traditional methods of tying the obi. Here, a method of tying the knot so that it may be tightened even after the hakama has been fully tied is presented. To make an adjustment, simply reach in through the sides of the hakama and pull on the loose ends of the obi below the *koshita* that is located behind the back.

TYING THE OBI

1: Begin with the *keigo-gi* or *montsuki* closed with the left front side crossed over the right.

2: Unfold a small tag end (hanging down in photo) of the *obi* and place it against the center of your stomach. Wrap the long end from left to right around the waist two times.

3: Place the end of the first wrap outside and over the wrapped section on the waist.

1-2: Continue to wrap the long section over the tag end and trap it between the outside and inside layers. Wrap once more around the waist. Pull the top of the short tag end up from between the two *obi* layers to create a small loop.

3: Measure the remaining end of the long section. Fold the long end to reduce the length. Trap the folded long and free end back under itself against the obi on the left side between the outside layer and the last wrap.

4: Pass the long end up through the small loop of the tag end.

5: Pull the long end over the tag end and forward.

6: Pass the forward long end down between the outermost wrap and next inner wrap. Pull down on both remaining ends to tighten the obi.

7: Begin turning the knot to the right clockwise around the waist.

8: As the knot circles the body, it tightens the *montsuki* as it rotates.

9: Finish with the knot in the back at the top of the hips.

No element of the budoka's uniform reveals or expresses his self-discipline more than the hakama. The care or neglect of the hakama is a good indication of his self-image and the depth of understanding of his role as a representative of the dojo and the ryu. When tying the hakama, begin with the keigo-gi or montsuki closed with the left front side crossed over the right. The obi should be securely tied with the knot turned to the back.

TYING THE HAKAMA

1: Unfold the *hakama* by pulling on the *himo* (strings).

2: Allow the back section of the hakama to drop down while holding on to the shorter front himo of the hakama. Step into the left leg of the hakama and then the right leg.

3: Place the top of the front panel near the top of the *obi* (belt).

CONTINUED ON NEXT PAGE

4: Wrap the long himo sections around the waist and cross them in the back over the knot tied in the *obi*. Continue to wrap both long ends of the himo around the body to the front. Straighten the himo to make sure they will lie flat.

5: Cross the long end over to form an X in front of the body approximately three inches below the bottom of the obi.

6: Wrap the loose ends around the back below the level of the obi.

7: Begin tying an overhand knot behind the back. The knot should lie beneath the knot on the obi.

8: Continue to tie a bow in the himo.

9: Lift the plastic *hera* that is attached to the inside back flap of the hakama and slip it over and between the layers of the obi.

10: Lift up the *koshita* (hip board) on the back of the hakama and position its bottom edge at the top edge of the obi and flat against the lower back.

11: Pull the short himo that are attached to the back of the hakama down at an angle toward the front.

12: Place the right himo end diagonally downward and cross over the X that was created by the first set of tied himo. Then cross the left himo over the right to form a second X.

CHAPTER 3

13: Tuck the outer most end of the himo under both X's and up through the center between the body of the hakama and both sets of himo.

14: Begin to tie a square knot by passing the uppermost loose end over the lower end. Then pass the vertical outer end up through the hole formed in the middle.

15: Tighten the square knot.

16: Fold the excess left end of the himo several times back against itself toward the knot.

17: Place the folded himo against the center knot and pull the loose-end himo downward into a vertical position.

18: Begin to wrap the lower loose himo around the folded section and the square knot. Bring the loose end up and over the folded himo and behind the square knot. Continue to wrap around the center section.

19: During the final pass, leave enough length on the himo to create a loop and pass it over the top of the center section and behind the knot. Allow the looped end to extend from below the knot and the final end to extend above the knot.

20: The final knot should form a "plus sign" at the front of the body. This knot resembles the Japanese *kanji* for the number 10 (*ju*).

If the uniform is properly stored and laundered, the budoka presents a dignified appearance and reveals an orderly mind. These actions should be considered and reflected on daily as part of polishing the technical skills and mental discipline needed to be ever ready for life's challenges. The idea behind it is that if a practitioner cannot defeat his own lazy tendencies, then mastery over any other aspect of life seems nearly impossible. Daily care will lengthen the life of the hakama and preserve its appearance for many years. Veteran budoka have spent countless hours seeing to the care of their uniform and folding the hakama. You might question why senior swordsmen would have spent more time in their lives folding their uniform than the novice has yet spent training on the dojo floor. These actions reflect back to the day when the constant preparation for training kept the samurai's mind and equipment ever ready for battle. "After the battle, tighten the helmets cords," was an admonition known to every samurai. It reminded him that he must be constantly prepared for the next encounter. Today, those same habits instill mindfulness and the quiet confidence in the practitioner's ability to act decisively at a moments notice.

HOW TO FOLD THE HAKAMA

Photos courtesy of Michael Gunshannon

1: Lay the *hakama* on a flat surface and straighten all of the pleats in the rear. Then flip the hakama over by holding all of the pleats at the bottom edge so they don't get mussed. Turn the hakama over and straighten the pleats on the front side of the hakama.

2: Fold the outer winged sides of the hakama inward toward the middle outer edge of the pleats.

3: Fold the bottom edge of the hakama upward in three sections to meet the top of the *koshita*.

4: Straighten the pair of long *himo* and fold them in half.

5: Then fold the himo against themselves once again. If they are very long, fold them in thirds.

6: The folded long himo ends lie close to the edge of the hakama.

7: Fold one long himo section diagonally across the hakama toward the opposite corner.

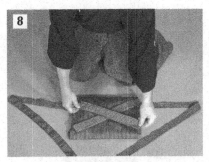

8: Fold the second long himo section diagonally across the first section toward the opposite corner.

9: Pass the short himo ends up and over the middle section of the crossed long himo ends. Pull the ends down behind the middle X.

10: Pull downward until the short himo lie flat against the folded long sections.

11: Pass both short himo ends around the lower leg ends of the long himo.

12: Fold one short himo end diagonally upward across the X and under the upper loop that encircles the long folded end.

13: Fold the remaining short himo end diagonally upward across the X and under the remaining upper loop that encircles the other long folded end.

14: Pull the short himo attached to the back of the hakama down at an angle toward the front.

15: The folded knot will resemble the wings of a butterfly.

The care and function of the uniform directly affects the support and function of the sword when it is worn on the body. Improper tightness of the obi will lead to restriction of movement or lack of support for the sword during the drawing process. Incorrect positioning of the hakama may lead to accidental tripping or constricted movement of the saya. If the *himo* are wrinkled or tangled because of improper folding the hakama will not fit properly nor will it maintain the correct position to facilitate wearing the sword comfortably. Once the fundamentals of caring for your uniform are assimilated, the actions of wearing and removing the sword can be addressed.

TAITO—WEARING THE SWORD

1: Begin with the sword held next to the hip in the left hand with the *sageo*, the string attached to the *saya,* looped between the index and middle fingers.

2: Reach under the sword with the right hand and transfer the sageo from your left hand to right hand. Grab the looped sageo between the ring finger and middle finger of the right hand.

3: Use the thumb of the left hand to find the outermost layer of the *obi* near the front of the body. Pull the layers apart with the left thumb.

4: Place the *kojiri* of the *saya* into the open layers of the obi with the assistance of the finger of left hand.

5: Push the sword into the obi with the right hand. As the ko-jiri exits the back of the obi, reach back with the left hand to grab the kojiri and pull the saya through. Stop when the right wrist makes contact with the center of the body. The inside of the *tsuba* should be on the centerline of the body.

6: Reach under the sword with the left hand and transfer the sageo to the left hand.

7: Pull back the sageo with the left hand and drape it over the top of the saya between the saya and the left hip at the point where the saya exits the obi.

8: Reach down with the left hand and pull the loose end of the sageo forward.

CONTINUED ON NEXT PAGE

Form a loop in the end of the sageo.

Pass the loop up behind the himo.

9: Transfer the end of the sageo to the right hand and form a loop. Tie the sageo onto the left side front *himo*.

10: Pull the sageo knot back to the left along the himo.

11: Secure the position of the sword on the body by aligning the tsuba in the center of the body and *tsuka gashira* forward to the right corner.

DATTO—REMOVING THE SWORD

1: To remove the sword from the *obi*, control the *tsuka gashira* with the right hand. Reach down with the left hand and find the *sageo* knot tied to the *hakama*.

2: Untie the knot by pulling downward on the free end with the left hand.

3: Grab the sageo with the left hand near the *kurigata* (sageo-retaining knob). Pull the sageo away from the body with the sageo held between the index and middle fingers of the left hand. Pull outward until there is one-third of the sageo hanging behind the hand.

4: Pull the left hand forward and form a hanging loop in the sageo. Grab the *saya* with the left hand as the thumb secures the *tsuba*.

5: Release the tsuka gashira with the right hand and push the sword forward with the left hand.

6: Take the sageo in the right hand between the ring and middle fingers. Grasp the saya with the right hand and secure the tsuba with the right index finger pointing forward. Pull the left hand back to the hip.

7: Push the sword forward out of the obi with the right hand.

8: Transfer the sageo to the left hand between the index and middle fingers. Grasp the saya with the left hand and secure the tsuba with the left thumb.

9: Lower the left hand and sword back to the left hip.

ETIQUETTE AND DOJO CONDUCT

Reiho (etiquette and manners) should be observed in every aspect of our lives if we wish to share the personal space of others. An old budo aphorism states, "An angry fist will not strike a smiling face." Though this may seem naïve to some, it exemplifies a conventional wisdom that diplomacy and kindness are the greatest means to achieving peace. The social structure within a dojo is no different. The need for conventional wisdom to be observed in an environment that is laced with mental, physical and sometimes emotional interaction should be apparent. The *dojo* is a forge. It is a place where you intentionally observe the fire that rises up within you. You train to eliminate the ignition point of your personality so that the enemy that stands before you no longer retains the power to strike the match that will bring down your house. But you do so with the greatest respect for one another in the process. It is reiho that allows the temperature of the dojo forge to rise higher and higher as your fellow practitioners stretch the boundaries of their comfort zones. The personal space that you invade during budo training reaches far beyond the normal borders of social proclivity. The reiho lubricates any of the friction that occurs in dojo relationships as you pass through training. It prevents you from igniting tempers or offending others.

New students often feel ignorant of the rituals and etiquette that are evident in the dojo. Lack of such information should not be considered as a lack of heart or sincerity. True etiquette comes from a good heart and it is not dampened by a lack of knowledge of physical actions. The teachers, parents and senior members of the community are there to guide and educate those with less experience in the social and culturally appropriate manners. *Shitsurei shimasu* is used in the Japanese language to precede a request when an inquiry is being made without the proper knowledge of propriety or inconvenience it may have to the recipient. Shitsurei establishes the understanding that the request comes from a "pure heart" that lacks the knowledge of the appropriate accompanying action.

Etiquette should be exercised for the benefit of others. The actions should not be performed in order to make a display or garner attention. The heart must be true for the action to come to life. All too often customs and courtesies are done by rote and without meaning. Adults frequently display perfunctory gestures that appear to be more of an inconvenience than a sign of respect. If the manners and actions lack the conviction of your intention, then they become an empty shell. This is considered *kyorei,* which is action without heart or sincerity. It is a representation of the least form of sincerity and respect for others. It is the act of knowing what is right and choosing disingenuousness. It is a form of dishonesty toward others and yourself.

Proper etiquette is essential as it signifies your commitment and appreciation for the cultural history of your sword art. Observation of etiquette indicates your sincerity and willingness to learn, and your trust and respect for the training space, your classmates and your instructors. Whether you are a beginner or an advanced student, you are equally responsible for following fundamental dojo manners. As a beginner, think of them as the first techniques to becoming a true budoka. If you have already been practicing for a while, think of these as a vital aspect of your striving for technical and personal perfection.

What is so important about dojo etiquette? In the days of the samurai, an inappropriate step or comment would have had immediate consequences. A wrong turn or misplaced weapon would ensure death on the battlefield. Attention to small details in daily life was preparation for all battlefield encounters. There are customs and traditions that have existed in the Japanese martial arts for centuries. Each came from the necessity to maintain battlefield competence, hierarchy and proper attitude toward one's seniors. In every dojo, there are seniors *(sempai),* and there are juniors *(kohai).* Each member must learn what role they play and where they are in the hierarchy of the dojo.

As we have previously noted, the teacher is the center of the dojo. Without the head instructor, there would be no group. He is the hub of the wheel that holds the dojo together, keeps the wheels turning and maintains the spirit and atmosphere. The teachers have already traveled the path you are on and are there to guide you along the way. Thus, all etiquette is set by the teacher's example.

The dojo is the room or the building or the spot where knowledge is passed from one generation to the next. It is a place where life changes occur. Therefore, the training space itself deserves respect and attention. Before entering the dojo training area, remove all hats, coats and shoes. No dojo member wants to have the dirt that your shoes have stepped in during the day to now be on the mat and, subsequently, on them and you. On entering, bow to the *kamiza* and sensei if he is in the dojo when you enter. This simple act acknowledges your instructor and his ability to teach you something you do not know. In doing so, you also acknowledge those who have spent their lives passing down the tradition. Thus, you acknowledge the warrior spirit that has passed through the generations to you.

Clean the dojo. Before class starts, it is the students' responsibility to make sure their training space is clean. Why does the student have to do this and not the teacher of the dojo? It is an act of gratitude and service. It begins to establish your personal relationship with your training space. Through this single act you are serving the dojo and ensuring its long life. Cleaning contributes to the welfare of your fellow students by giving them a clean environment. It builds camaraderie and contributes to establishing your place in the group.

If it is unavoidable that you arrive late for class, dress quickly and wait near the *shimoza* for permission to join the group. Speak softly and move quietly so as not to draw attention away from the instruction.

Simplicity is the mark of traditional Japanese sword arts. The training uniform should reflect this. Each member of the dojo is expected to fit in. Jewelry, patches or other adornments that stand out will only draw attention that is inappropriate to the training. Be sure your training uniform is clean before every class. Hygiene is a sign of your respect for yourself and others. The relationships in a dojo are closer than most anywhere else you may encounter. Close body contact is inevitable and your concern for others' comfort should be a priority. Maintain proper grooming and well-trimmed finger nails. Be sure that the training uniform ensures modesty and does not reveal too much.

Training weapons should be well-maintained. When transporting equipment outside of the dojo, a gear bag and weapons case should be used. While in the dojo, it is imperative to respect the training equipment of others. Do not step on or over a sword or other weapon. When placing weapons on a rack or near the wall, be sure to point the cutting edge away from the *shomen.* Do not stand weapons against the wall where they can topple or fall over. When training has ended, be sure to return all weapons to their proper storage.

While training, refrain from stepping in front of others, especially when two partners are performing kumitachi. Whether others are engaged in training or not, always try to walk behind a line of members in the dojo rather than cross between them and the shomen. However, do not walk behind someone swinging a sword! Wait until they have ceased their movements, then request permission to pass.

Always show proper respect for training partners. Juniors and seniors must respect the spirit and space or their comrades in arms. Listen to the teacher's instructions and direction. It is improper to question the instructions or critique of a senior even if it appears to be in contrast to what you believe to be true. Always wait for the teacher to be near you before requesting a clarification or correction. Do not call from across the dojo to a teacher or other student. If necessary, walk over to them and express regret for the interruption and permission to address the issue.

Tolerance is one of the marks of a senior member of the dojo. Learn to accept criticism and direction with humility and gratitude. Maintain the spirit of a true warrior while training. Budo is difficult. Injuries and hardships occur. The reality of combat is no different. Learn to accept stress, fatigue and injury with decorum and dignity. These obstacles should be accepted as the fires that temper the metal of the swordsman.

When class is dismissed, perform the proper bow to the shomen and teacher before exiting the floor. It is the senior students' responsibility to teach their juniors the proper etiquette and appropriate behavior expected in the dojo. Each senior member should assume the responsibility for instructing new members in the actions that will allow them to fit in. Kindness and compassion should be shown at all times, and the instructions should be given as constructive guidance.

DEGREE OF ETIQUETTE

The most informal form of the bow is the *eshaku-rei* or the *moku-rei* (no voice). This 15-degree bow is used to convey a greeting to friends or people you are familiar with. Eshaku-rei is the bow performed before *embu* (demonstration). Moku-rei is a basic bow used to say "hello" to a friend or colleague. The moku-rei should be performed without any verbalization. Moku-rei means "a bow with no words" whereas the term eshaku-rei refers to the actual act of bowing at 15 degrees. It is considered inappropriate to use the shallow form of bowing if a deeper bow is more appropriate to the situation.

ESHAKU-REI

1: Begin with the sword held in the right hand with the edge of the blade facing down. The *saya kojiri* points forward at 45 degrees.

2: Maintain good posture with the shoulders back and head erect. Keep the back straight and lean forward to a 15-degree angle. Breathe in as you begin to bow. The back of the head, shoulders and hips should remain in a straight line. The *metsuke* (eye's visual plane) lowers downward as the body inclines forward. Breathe out at the bottom of the bow. Hold this position for one full second.

3: After one second, breathe in and begin to rise. Return to the upright position.

The 30-degree bow *(shi-rei)* is used to convey a deeper expression of appreciation. The bow is held longer than the eshaku-rei and is used when addressing teachers or seniors. It is also performed when requesting a favor or addressing a delicate situation. It is the most common bow used.

SHI-REI—30-DEGREE BOW

1: Begin with the sword held in the right hand with the edge of the blade facing down. The *saya kojiri* points forward at 45 degrees.

2: Maintain good posture with the shoulders back and head erect. Breathe in as you begin to bow. Keep the back straight and lean forward to a 30-degree angle. The back of the head, shoulders and hips should remain in a straight line. The *metsuke* (eye's visual plane) lowers downward as the body inclines forward. Breathe out and hold this position for two full seconds.

3: After two seconds, breathe in and begin to rise slowly. Return to the upright position.

The 45- to 90-degree bow is used to convey the deepest expression of sincerity and gratitude. The bow is held longer than the shi-rei and is used for ceremonial occasions to show the deepest veneration or humility, like when bowing to the dojo kamiza. *Hai-rei* is also performed when offering a very sincere apology or expressing condolences in delicate situations. It is the most sincere bow used.

HAI-REI (OGAMU)—45- TO 90-DEGREE BOW

1: Begin with the sword held in the right hand with the edge of the blade facing down. The *saya kojiri* points forward and down at 45 degrees.

2: Maintain good posture with the shoulders back and head erect. Breathe in as you begin to bow. Keep the back straight and lean forward to a 90-degree angle. The back of the head, shoulders and hips should remain in a straight line. The *metsuke* (eye's visual plane) lowers downward as the body inclines forward. Breathe out and hold this position for three full seconds. Do not lower the chin far enough to allow the back of the neck to be seen from the front.

3: After three seconds, breathe in and begin to rise slowly. Return to the upright position.

THE FORMAL PRACTICE OF REIHO

The first two ceremonial performances of Eishin-ryu practice entail the formal acknowledgment and respect for the great contributions that have been passed down for generations. The dojo represents many environmental aspects of a practitioner's life, such as was discussed in the previous chapter of the relationship between the swordsman and his tradition and the student-teacher bond. All of the practitioner's feelings about these relationships are summed up in the physical acts of *hai-rei* and *shi-rei*. They are the outward manifestations that affect the mind of the swordsman as he prepares to embark on a passage of discovery to deepen his understanding of the toho (sword method).

To learn efficiently, a proper attitude must be observed in your heart. Respect for your environment shows a deep understanding of the nature of budo. Hai-rei is the outward manifestation of your sincere respect and gratitude for the environment and shi-rei is the confirmation of gratitude for your teacher and the teachings that are about to be made available to you. Both hai-rei and shi-rei are to be performed as described in the following instructions. *Hai-rei* should be performed while facing the shomen or *kamidana*.

Shi-rei should be performed while facing your teacher.

HAI-REI AND SHI-REI

1: Begin with the sword held in the left hand near the hip with the edge of the blade facing up.

2: Reach across with the right hand as the sword is pushed forward with the left hand.

3: Bring the sword forward and hold the *tsuba* at shoulder height. Grasp the *sageo* with the right hand between the ring and middle fingers.

4: Turn the right wrist counterclockwise as if you are looking at a wristwatch. Grasp the *saya* just below the tsuba with the right hand. As the right hand approaches the saya, collect the loosely hanging sageo loops and pin them against the saya with your outward turned right thumb and palm.

5: Rotate the right wrist and saya counterclockwise.

6: Release the left hand from the saya and begin to lower the right hand and saya to the right side. Control the lateral movement of the saya by placing the right-hand index finger on the *mune* section of the saya.

CONTINUED ON NEXT PAGE

7: Hold the sword at the right side of the body at arm's length with the right index finger pointing the *kojiri* forward and down at a 45-degree angle.

8: Bow at 45 to 90 degrees in the direction of the *shomen* (dojo front) or *kamidana* (spirit shelf) to perform *hai-rei,* or toward your teacher at 30 degrees to perform *shi-rei.*

9: After three seconds, breathe in and begin to rise. Return to the upright position.

The actions of the sword are a reflection of the intentions within the heart of the swordsman who wields it. It may be a sword that takes life or one that preserves life. The samurai held the sword in high regard as an object of truth and power. *To-rei* is the act of acknowledging the spirit of the sword and demonstrating your respect for its integrity and careful use.

In the beginning of a practice session, after bowing to the teacher, the sword practitioner performs a bow to the sword. At the end of practice, the sword is shown respect first. The initial to-rei usually begins following the hai-rei and shi-rei. The instructions listed here begin from the final position taken after the first two bows have been completed.

TO-REI—BOW TO THE SWORD

1: Begin with the sword held in the right hand with the edge of the blade facing down. The *saya kojiri* points forward at 45 degrees.

2: Raise the right hand and rotate the right wrist counter-clockwise toward the chest with your elbow at shoulder height as if looking at a wristwatch on the right wrist.

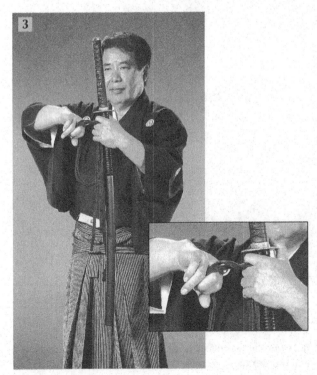

3: Grasp the *sageo*, near the *tsuba*, with the index and middle fingers of the left hand.

4: Release the right hand from the sageo and lift the tsuba to the left at shoulder height using the left hand. Support the opposite end of the *saya* from underneath with the palm of the right hand. The cutting edge of the sword faces inward toward the body.

CONTINUED ON NEXT PAGE

5: Lift the sword with both hands to forehead height. The cutting edge faces the top of the forehead and the tsuka points to the left.

6: Perform *to-rei* at 30 degrees to show respect to the sword.

7: After three seconds, return to a vertical position.

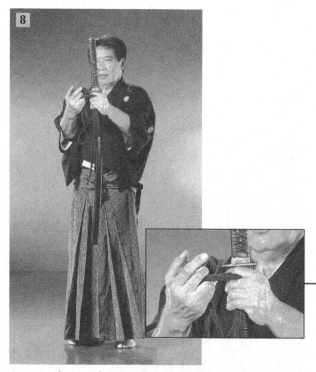

8: Lower the sword to a vertical position in front of the body and transfer the sageo into the right hand. Grasp the sageo between the ring and middle fingers of the right hand.

9: Grasp the saya with the right hand. Slide the left hand down to the saya and examine the *mekugi* in the tsuka. The eyes should focus forward past the sword held at face level.

10: Lower the left hand to the saya kojiri and pull the *kojiri* back to the top of the *obi* at the left hip to establish *taito* (wearing the sword).

CHAPTER 4

PRINCIPLES OF
JAPANESE SWORDSMANSHIP

Both the modern and ancient forms of kenjutsu contain certain principles and concepts that are easily recognized by experienced swordsman. These fundamental technical aspects and principles are the quintessence of the swordsman's function and effectiveness. Even though various styles of kenjutsu and battojutsu have developed, the following characteristics have come to be the defining aspects that are judged and evaluated in order to determine a swordsman's *fukaku*, which refers to his depth of understanding and the spectrum of his ability.

SHISEI—POSTURE

Natural movement comes from relaxation and the correct structural alignment of the body. The most fundamental rule for maintaining a proper posture is to hold the body vertically erect. The top of the head should be directly centered over the shoulders and the middle of the hips at all times. The shoulders and hips form a vertically upright rectangle as the body moves horizontally in any plane. This vertically centered position allows for the body to maintain balance and stability. With the body stable and balanced, mobility is easily controlled.

As the body moves, the vertical plane must be supported by the structure of the legs and feet. The bipod that they form with the hips reinforces all of the upper body's structure. Kenjutsu movements are executed by converting the body's weight that is pressing against the ground into energy that travels back up into the hips and creates a supported structure known as *iaigoshi*. Iaigoshi refers to the "carry" of the hips during the performance of kenjutsu and battojutsu.

In order for the body to move horizontally under equilibrium and balance, its weight must first be transferred downward and then propelled laterally from foot to foot. This transfer of energy occurs between the hips. The body's weight presses downward against the ground as the muscle and skeletal structure of the feet and legs forces energy to travel back up through the knees and into the hips to propel them forward or back. This upward spiral of energy supports the torso and shoulders in all techniques and movements. The more the upper body relaxes, the more stability is created in the lower bipod and platform that is created by the hips, legs and feet. This allows more energy to be pushed back up into the hips.

An essential element of this iaigoshi is learning to create stasis between the upper body and lower bipod. The weight of the body traveling downward must be countered by the energy of the feet, knees and legs pushing upward. The upper head and torso must remain erect while the lower body moves on any horizontal plane. Any motion of the upper body that upsets its vertical plane forces the legs to change the direction of upwardly moving energy in order to support the unbalanced position. This is energy that is lost for the purpose of powerful technique.

As complicated as this may sound, it is your natural state of propulsion. Walking requires you to push against the ground to force your hips and torso forward. The energy must cross the centerline of the hips each time this occurs. The upper body only needs to be supported naturally by the spine and lower torso.

It is important to maintain this upright alignment of the back, neck and head regardless of the *kamae*. Whether you are drawing and cutting, slashing or thrusting, both iaigoshi and straight spinal alignment must be maintained for optimum balance, speed and power. When proper posture is displayed during waza, the structure of the body becomes energized and alive. The body and sword move together in harmony and dignity.

KOKYU—BREATH

Breath gives life to the technique. The breath energizes the blood and expels toxins on exhalation. Controlled breathing can be used to lighten or condense the weight of the body during a technique. Breath control is a critical skill that every sword practitioner must develop.

Speed, timing and execution of power are all affected by how you control the rate and degree of your breathing. Shallow breathing patterns cause the center of balance to rise into the upper torso and create instability and loss of equilibrium. The muscles of the shoulders begin to contract and relaxation in swinging the sword becomes difficult if not impossible. In contrast, correct deep-breathing techniques slow the rush of adrenaline, if the mind and emotions are brought under control. As the body relaxes, the center of balance adjusts to the lower body and additional oxygen is supplied to fuel the blood and respiratory system.

Fukushiki kokyu is an exercise that may be practiced as preparation to relax the body and quiet the mind before each waza. Although it is not regularly practiced as a part of the Eishin-ryu batto-ho waza, which will be introduced later in this book, it is a regimented requisite in the older koryu forms. This breathing exercise prepares the mind and body for relaxed and continuous movement. Within the *koryu waza*, the initial breathing pattern is established in the following manner:

Stand upright in a natural posture with the arms relaxed at the sides. Inhale through the nostrils as the air is drawn in and up around the top of the head. Imagine the air moving downward along the spine and accumulating in the lower abdomen on *tanden*. As the air appears to dissipate throughout the body, exhale naturally. The air that is inhaled actually inflates the lungs. The mental image of circulating this air allows the diaphragm to draw air deeper into the lungs and supply more oxygen to the body. Take a second breath while following the same procedure. Allow the body to relax as the mind becomes energized and active. This reduction of tension calms the nervous system and allows the muscles to respond faster.

The procedure for the third breath varies depending on your experience and the level of studied training. During *shoden*-level training, the hands begin to perform the initial steps of drawing the sword on the third inhalation. The exhalation of the third breath is completed at the end of nukitsuke. While performing fukushiki kokyu in the performance of *okuden waza*, the third inhalation is held until the end of the final kirioroshi. Although breath control is necessary for maintaining and maximizing power, balance and stamina during combat, there is greater benefit to the mental and emotional state of the swordsman.

Negative thoughts and emotions are displaced by proper breathing and thought patterns. While inhaling and exhaling, the mind should begin to perceive the manifestation of the environment as it unfolds.

Unconstructive thoughts and fears are erased, and the circumstances represented in the waza are allowed to be experienced as they unfold. Each moment that passes is drawn into the body along with the third inhalation. The first movement of the sword is created by the mind's intention to fit into the picture that is quietly revealing itself. This mental cleansing is referred to as *jaki o dasu*.

DATSU-RYOKU—RELAXED POWER

Waza is the basic level of repetitive training in budo in which you study how to execute movement and technique. At this level of practice, the mind works consciously, telling the practitioner to "put energy here" or perhaps "push or move there." In short, the thinking mind directs each action that you execute. Jutsu is the natural expression of technique—the embodiment of toho—there is no thinking during the execution of an action. Through constant practice of waza in the dojo, it is hoped that the practitioner will come to a point where his technique manifests naturally from inside; this is jutsu.

To understand and accomplish the progression from waza to jutsu, you must learn how to relax. In budo, instructors constantly admonish students to relax in order to move the body freely, utilizing whole body power. This principle is referred to as *datsu-ryoku*. One key element of datsu-ryoku (relaxed power) stems from correct posture, which then allows for proper balance. If you are unbalanced, your body will be tense as it attempts to compensate for the lack of balance. In short, imbalance impedes relaxation. Muscular tension is also a major impediment to datsu-ryoku and, therefore, jutsu. You need to train to let go of such tension. A good example is found in how the *tsuka* is grasped during *tsuka no nigiri kata*. If the grip is too hard, muscular and mental tension is created, which inhibits the ability to swing the sword properly and cut efficiently. Under such conditions, jutsu cannot be expressed in the attempt to cut. Correct posture and the elimination of muscular tension are the major components of datsu-ryoku, which then makes jutsu possible. This is a major principle of all martial arts.

To expand on the idea of datsu-ryoku and its relevance to waza and jutsu, use the analogy of lifting and donning *yoroi* (armor). Yoroi can be somewhat heavy and cumbersome. If you were to pick up yoroi for the first time, your mind would note that the yoroi is heavy and would signal the muscles to prepare for the action of lifting a heavy weight. The body tenses and a great deal of muscle is used to lift the armor. This is equivalent to the practice of waza. However, if you don the yoroi, it becomes supported by the structure of your body. Very quickly, it seems that the armor is not so heavy after all. The mind begins to assign less importance to the heaviness of the yoroi, and the mind and body begin to relax. After a while, you forget that you are wearing armor and begin to move around in a natural and relaxed way. This is waza leading to jutsu through datsu-ryoku.

Datsu-ryoku and jutsu are frequently expressed in everyday actions of advanced budo practitioners. It can be seen even in such mundane actions as lifting a heavy object. He who understands datsu-ryoku will utilize "extension" in the lift. This expression of datsu-ryoku in movement is essential in battojutsu. All battojutsu movement is expressed with the entire body, enabling the practitioner to express jutsu in his or her practice. Developing your ability beyond waza to the relaxed expression of jutsu, enables your mind to relax further. The relaxation of the mind and the elimination of conscious thought through battojutsu practice may also enable you to enter a sort of meditative state, a sort of "moving Zen" that contributes to the health of the spirit as well as that of the mind and body.

METSUKE—EYE CONTACT

The physical sense that is primary in combat is that of sight. Vision provides people with intelligence about their environment at the speed of light. The only handicap is in processing the information fast enough to take advantage of an opportunity when it is presented.

If you fix your gaze on a single element of an event, then your mind processes the information that is its main focus. This ability serves you well in scenarios where attention to minute details is needed and distractions are best blocked out. However, it's not advantageous under battlefield conditions where multiple angles of attack present constant danger. For these conditions, it is more suitable to fix your gaze on the field of vision that takes in the most space. That is not to say that the opponent directly before you is not considered a threat. Instead, widening the field of view makes it possible to respond to the tiniest movements while processing information from the entire battlefield.

This was imperative for samurai to survive attacks on a crowded field of combat. All manner of weapons and artillery were to be observed even while they struck down the immediate threat. This method of viewing combat was referred to as *enzan no metsuke*, which means "viewing the distant mountains." The swordsman does not fix his gaze directly on the opponent. The *metsuke* (eye position) is directed on the opponent but the field of view is not limited to him. Peripheral vision widens and captures all movement within 180 degrees around the body. The metsuke is directed at the opponent and beyond, which allows the swordsman's field of view to capture sword movements coming from all directions. Enzan no metsuke is critical in situations against multiple opponents. It enables you to see the "big picture." Viewing in this way allows a combatant to be able to take in the entire environment. He is able to see and feel emerging conditions while being aware of the potential for other adversaries. Enzan no metsuke should only be applied in situations where you face multiple opponents in a martial encounter. By understanding this, you can infer that it should not be applied in waza where you presumably face only one opponent or in practice of some kumitachi.

Instead, metsuke is applied in other ways. In a face-to-face confrontation with a single opponent, metsuke is constantly changing. The eye's focus can move from the opponent's eyes to his hips, shoulders, hands or chest. Because your gaze is never fixed, you aren't deceived by an opponent's feints or deceptions nor would you be trapped by the fear that the opponent's power or eye contact might inspire. Some styles advocate watching the hips or the legs to avoid the possibility of feeling this fear. Other traditions advocate watching the eyes or the hands of an opponent. The eyes, while a source of the expression of kihaku, can also give away an opponent's intent, and generally, the intent in the eyes is rarely misleading whereas, when watching an opponent's hand, it is unlikely that the opponent will attack if the hand does not move.

Metsuke is often dependent on an opponent's kamae. In these cases, the metsuke must shift to the eyes, shoulders or chest. Metsuke should not be limited to watching one or two parts of the opponent. It cannot be stressed enough that your metsuke must continue to move. The mind must be still but never stuck despite the constant shifting of the metsuke.

Correct eye contact involves reading the opponent's movement. It also involves reading his kamae. In fact, to be successful, metsuke is often dependent upon the opponent's kamae. For example, if the opponent moves into *jodan no kamae* or *waki no kamae*, watching his hand may be unreliable. This is very important, because good metsuke and a correct understanding of kamae enables you to know what the opponent will do next. It will often be evident whether he is going to draw or how he intends to attack.

It is also important to understand that complete metsuke is not limited to vision. Correct metsuke utilizes all senses, including your so-called "sixth sense" in which you apply "*kan no mi*"—the ability to read the opponent's mind and to feel or detect his intent. Good eye contact allows a feel for an opponent's *ki,* which may manifest as a physical sensation. To understand metsuke, it is important to be familiar with *zanshin,* which will be explored presently.

All too often, new sword practitioners perform their waza with what is known as "dead eyes." There is little in their eyes that would signify that they are facing an opponent. Nothing in their countenance indicates that they understand metsuke. If there is a lack of focus, there can be no metsuke or kihaku. To develop proper metsuke in sword waza, it is vitally important to use your imagination to see the opponent. Try to imagine an opponent during practice. The opponent needs to be at the appropriate distance, three or four feet, to make the waza as real as possible. Another way to develop proper metsuke is to practice paired waza frequently.

KIHAKU—ENERGIZED INTENT

The technical aspects of kenjutsu are the outward manifestations of a greater power. The seat of this power rests in the mind and spirit *(kokoro)*. The mind holds the power to construct the strategy, tactics and determination necessary to complete your missions in battle and in life. All things created by man first exist as potentiality in the mind. The technical aspects of sword manipulation are little more than the physical realization of your thoughts.

Intention emanates from the potential of formulated thoughts. If you wish to lift an arm, the brain creates an intention that enables you to do so. The intense energy needed to deliver movement with commitment and determination is enhanced by confidence in your knowledge and actions. Kihaku is a combination of willpower, confidence in ability and knowledge that a cause is righteous and just. It is righteousness within the mind of the swordsman that enables his mind, body and spirit to unite in a coordinated effort to conquer fear and energize his performance with spirit and power.

Spirit should be evident from the moment the swordsman steps onto the dojo floor. It should not be confused with arrogance even though the stature of the swordsman may reflect some similarity. Movements that reflect kihaku reveal themselves to be bursting with dignity and confidence. They are devoid of any apparent fear for your survival over the commitment to accomplish an objective. There is power and righteousness that radiates from the waza. In fact, the energy seems to drive the waza itself. When kihaku is present within technique, the intention of the technique comes alive and the spirit of the technique becomes palpable. Presence of this spirited energy displays itself in every attitude the swordsman assumes.

As noted with metsuke, the eyes are a window that projects the energy, willpower and fierce determination of a swordsman who is committed not to fail throughout the waza and *katachi*. Without this kihaku, the actions and even the appearance of the warrior become lifeless. The kihaku that is evident in advanced practitioners is the result of arduous training. It cannot be achieved overnight. The confidence and knowledge that your technique is capable and ready for action at all times is a prerequisite. A forged and tempered fighting spirit can only be attained by facing tough training partners that push you to your limits and beyond. It is a result of having faced many opponents and multitudes of scenarios over and over again. Kihaku cannot be based on false confidence. Bravado and machismo play no role in truly expressing kihaku. A true fighting spirit and its intensely focused energy is the offspring of hard training and the sincere belief that your actions and motives are just.

JO HA KYU—MODULATION OF MOVEMENT

Those who are familiar with Japanese performance arts will recognize a certain timing and speed with which the performance presents itself. Elements of the individual techniques as well as the overall story being portrayed are established in a crescendo that pushes the performance. Battojutsu techniques also incorporate this modulation of intent and timing within the overall waza and the individual kihon. The techniques begin as though the intention is building within the body's movement. The collection of intention and the commencement of movement is referred to as *jo* (the beginning). As committed intention progressively adds tension and weight to the technique, it begins to crack or tear through any barrier that defines it as stillness or non-action. The breaking away of the barrier that separates the action and non-action is a modulation referred to as *ha*.

During this stage of movement, the technique is propelled against the body's natural tendency to remain at rest. The mind's intention becomes heavier than nature's ability to hold the body back. As a technique is pressured into the space that exists between the two combatants, the mind and body are drawn in by a gravity that builds between the adversaries. As the barrier that separates non-action from action fractures and explodes, the technique rushes in and occupies the space between the combatants in a great explosion of energy known as *kyu*. The timing and transition through *jo ha kyu* is a natural acceleration from non-action to a great crescendo of action. The speed of the technique accelerates from slow to fast, culminating in an explosive finale.

The components of each technique within the waza are performed with this feeling of jo ha kyu. It is evident when nukitsuke is performed. The energy and intention formulates the first part of the draw and intensifies as the *kissaki* approaches the *koiguchi*. As the energy breaks through the opponent's will to cease his action, the kissaki cuts through the koiguchi and moves into its final *hasuji*. This is the breaking or ha stage of the cut. The timing and action from saya banare to the final finish, as the sword accelerates and the will to cut modulates aggressively, is the transition to kyu. This transition and modulation of intensity and speed is enacted in kirioroshi and chiburi as well. The feeling is like inflating a balloon until the inevitable explosion finally occurs in each technique.

Waza should also reflect this principle of jo ha kyu as it passes through nukitsuke to the final kirioroshi, chiburi and noto. The speed, timing and intensity of the waza should continue to build as it tells the story from the beginning to the climactic end.

MAAI—DISTANCE

Japanese sword arts place great emphasis on the understanding of *ma*, which constitutes the space of things. All things that have form also have ma. In Western culture, personal ma is the space that is occupied when comfortably extending our hands in any direction around us. Personal comfort within a defined space differs from culture to culture and varies with societal relationships. The understanding of personal space in relationships dictates your ability to move about unencumbered and unaffected by the personal space of others. The space that exists between two objects is the *maai*. *Ma* is the ideographic *kanji* for space and *ai* is the representation for the concept of harmony or fitting in. Therefore maai is the space that intersects with the space of another.

The distance that is of most concern to warriors is combative space. In this book, this term signifies the space that separates two swordsmen as they attempt to control the distance between them during combat. Eishin-ryu techniques take advantage of many changing aspects of maai. Maai is not just the relative distance and space that is needed when cutting with the sword. It is the spatial relationship that always exists between the combatants. It is dynamic and continually reestablishes itself during the onslaught of battle in regard to cutting distance, blocking distance, grappling distance, etc.

Traditionally the first set of waza or katachi taught in koryu methods of instruction address the maai involved at longer distances. It is believed that the understanding of the most expanded combative space must be mastered before engaging in close-range combat. Greater distance corresponds to more time. By practicing the waza and kumitachi that offer engagements at longer ranges, the swordsman is given additional time to react and respond to the engagement with his opponent. Beginners require this additional time to respond and develop large technique. It is for this reason that shoden-level techniques are done slower and stress large movements.

The second exploration of maai is usually undertaken at the *chuden* level of training. At this stage in training, close-range scenarios are encountered. Closer distances coincide with shorter times to react and less space to maneuver. New methods of *tai-sabaki* are introduced that enable the escaping and controlling of the enemy's attacks. Maai at these close ranges often include grappling and are the inspiration for many jujutsu techniques.

The third maai studied is the relationship the swordsman has with multiple opponents on the battlefield. Fighting multiple opponents requires a deeper understanding of strategy and tactics. In truth, this understanding comes as a byproduct of the experience you gain during shoden and chuden initiations into maai. Battlefield combat against multiple opponents requires a swordsman to develop the ability to sense all threats and prioritize the dangers and opportunities that each offers. Against multiple attackers, it is necessary to observe each and every one of the opponents as a single unit, just as you would observe the limbs of an individual's entire body. Each unit is comprised of a right and left flank in addition to a main body. The combative space that the unit is able to control is dependent on its mobility and access to their opponent. Enzan no metsuke and zanshin is crucial to the awareness of the maai in this situation. Each time the group moves as a unit or individuals move within the group, the combative space changes and the tactics must change with it. It is wise to visualize the group of opponents as a single body with right and left arms that may choose to attack from either side or attempt to surround and capture. The maai is then treated as though you're facing a single enemy at a greater distance. While practicing okuden waza, the sword should feel as though it is always cutting into the next threat even as it is moving through its present target. The intent and spirit of the swordsman precedes the sword and continues to cut through the body and limbs of the enemy ahead of the actual physical movement. This cutting through with the kihaku and spirit establishes control of the maai between you and the next opponent even before the sword is physically occupying the space.

Once the ability to control the maai with multiple attackers is understood, the combative space engaged in while facing a single opponent becomes clearer. Each of the angles of attack and defense offer greater opportunity. The relationship between distance and timing learned during multiple-attack scenarios produces new targets and the ability to move slower, even within closer distances than previously thought. The aggressive fighting spirit developed to control the maai of *okuden*-level attacks establishes an offensive state of mind that involuntarily wishes to seize control of the combative space. When facing an opponent with this type of controlling spirit, the force of his will is present within the maai even before his body or sword enter. At this stage of understanding, the maai can be felt at huge distances. The greater the power of the combatant's fighting spirit, the larger the battlefield and combative space becomes. In many ways, the maai of two accomplished swordsman is not measured by the *kiri-ma*—the distance from which they can strike one another with swords—but instead it is measured by the distance that they can affect each other's spirits and wrest control of the combative space before the physical engagement begins.

SEME—PRESSURE

Seme, or pressure, should be exerted against the opponent's spirit and will to win. The combative distance is first controlled by the intention of the swordsman. He must display the determination and willpower to cut through anything that stands within the reach of his sword. The enemy should never be given the opportunity to think about anything other than defending himself. This includes making the opponent constantly wary of allowing an opening in his defense. Certainly the determination to win starts in the mind but it must also have physical manifestations, as well.

The sword must always be in the process of cutting. This means that even between movements and while seemingly stationary in kamae, the swordsman is cutting some target area on his opponent. The cutting edge should always be alive. The intention and energy that is established in the mind should always extend outward through the cutting edge. New practitioners to battojutsu or kenjutsu often find themselves caught off-guard or trying to catch up to the opponent's movements. At times, even some advanced practitioners discover that they are rushed to complete the next blocking or cutting movement. This is because of a lack of seme. Experienced budoka never appear to be rushed. There is something present that, even though they appear to move slower than their opponent, their sword finds it mark sooner. That something is pressure. They are cutting through the adversary at all times. If the sword is always cutting the enemy, then there is no need to hurry. It is the opponent that must work harder to not get cut.

An accomplished swordsman will also learn to test his opponent's *fudoshin* (immovable spirit). Fudoshin is the ideal mindset in which none of the four sicknesses are able to take root. These four sicknesses are fear, doubt, surprise and captivation *(kyo ku gi waku)*. When any of these sicknesses in the opponent are perceived, he is susceptible to attack. When these weaknesses are present in the enemy, the astute swordsman must apply 100-percent commitment to cut down his foe. To identify any of these weaknesses, a trained fencer will pressure his opponent's left hand to see if it is moving or still. It is said that a disturbed left hand in swordsmanship reflects an unfocused mind. His left hand reflects his mind and spirit, and his right hand reveals his technique or strategy.

Another method of testing the enemy's resolve is to pressure against his kissaki in order to test his attitude. It's possible to do this by performing what is known as "throwing roof tiles against the castle gate."

This refers to a samurai scout who would be recruited to gather intelligence about the conditions of the enemy's fortifications. He would occasionally throw stones or old roof tiles against the fortified gates to ascertain the spirit of the castle by the response elicited. Once the spirit of the castle was determined, the scout's job was finished. The swordsman does the same. The tip of the sword is used as a "scouting sword" to qualify whether there is a fighting spirit in the opponent's sword or if the fortification is spiritless. Pressure the enemy into divulging his weaknesses and strengths. If his resolve or technique is devoid of spirit or weak, rush in and cut down at him decisively. If there is strategy within the enemy's kamae, then attempt to draw it out. Create pressure that will make him change his current attitude. If the opponent changes his position or attitude, he has fallen ill to one of the four sicknesses. He has doubted his kamae and expressed fear of being cut. At this moment, you will have pressured and captured his spirit and will now attempt to occupy his space.

Pressure can also be launched against the opponent's technique. The opponent can be pressured into acting defensively or offensively. This combative pressure requires strong spirit and initiative. Do not allow the enemy to express his spirit through his technique. Cut down and through the opponent's sword when he attempts to cut you. This is the primary strategy of the *Itto-ryu* school of swordsmanship. The enemy's spirit is never allowed to be expressed within your combative space. Whoever exerts the most pressure and enters the battleground committed to winning will emerge victorious.

ZANSHIN—AWARENESS

Awareness or *zanshin* can be thought of as the accumulated information already processed by the brain as well as the presence of your character and spirit within the current environment. It is not enough to simply be an observer in world. To exhibit zanshin, the practitioner must also be a spiritual participant who adds to the character of the environment. It is an experiential existence. A true sense of zanshin is only possible if the practitioner is living at his highest life potential. A warrior with zanshin should never be caught off-guard. To be so would be contradictory to the very definition of the word. Warriors who develop zanshin have an innate sense of their surroundings and the ability to reach out into the environment to capture information that others might find insignificant or irrelevant. The ever present need for more information is why zanshin appears to be most present at the end of technique. The mind remains present and hungry. It searches for more information that will satisfy its need to analyze events and perceive any change as it occurs.

Lingering awareness is truly the prerequisite for all that defines a practitioner of battojutsu. To perform battojutsu properly means to be ever present and in harmony with the environment. Throughout the performance of batto, the practitioner needs "to fit exactly within one's environment." So to practice battojutsu is to exist with your full presence and fit within the moment. This is only possible through zanshin. The development of this awareness is considered paramount to becoming a master level budoka. This state of awareness is free of fear, worry, emotion and prejudice. It exemplifies the state of heijoshin. To exist in a state of peaceful coexistence with ones environment the mind must be actively acknowledging changes that occur while remaining undisturbed by the circumstances presented. This lingering mind and spirit, zanshin, is allowed to fill all of the emptiness that seems to exist when change becomes imperceptible.

CHAPTER 5

FUNDAMENTAL TECHNIQUES
OF JAPANESE SWORDSMANSHIP

Kihon (fundamentals) are the underlying characteristics of all kenjutsu techniques. They were developed to protect and serve the samurai in his daily chores and while performing his duties for his family and his country. The myriad kihon were formulated to deal with intricacies of nukitsuke (drawing the sword), kiritsuke (cutting), ukete (blocking), tai-sabaki (stepping and turning), chiburi (cleaning the blade) and noto (resheathing the sword) to name but a few.

There is no end to the practice of these kihon. It is the amalgamation of good kihon techniques that allows the waza to work. The constant improvement of the basic techniques and movements allows the energy to be used to its maximum efficiency. Continuous refinement of the kihon will produce greater speed, power, control and heijoshin. This chapter places great emphasis on the small things, for it is the small things that make the difference between a novice and a master.

KAMAE—ATTITUDE AND POSTURE

Posture and attitude are defining elements in Japanese budo. Without these two aspects of structure and mindset, there can be no connection to the sword. Despite the need for structure and attitude, there are no contrived stances in Eishin-ryu sword style. This is one of the infinite paradoxes in kenjutsu. It puts great emphasis on correct posture and attitude, but at the same time, it stresses that stances are natural. Therefore kamae is essentially nonexistent.

The literal meaning or translation of kamae is "structure or attitude." It is not only a physical posture but a physical, mental and emotional presence that is represented through the body's structure and relative position. It is a method of giving life to a practitioner's structure in preparation to being able to take advantage of offensive or defensive opportunities when they present themselves. Kamae are dynamic in that they constantly change and adapt to the environment as it presents itself anew. The structure and attitude of each kamae adjusts and transitions to the next kamae in accordance with the swordsman's need to complement or place pressure on the position of his enemy. Kamae is always alive with the emotional and mental state of the swordsman. To study an enemy's kamae is to reach deeply within his inner being in order to ascertain his greatest strengths and weaknesses.

When asked about the meaning of kamae, most martial arts practitioners typically define kamae as "combative posture." While this is correct on a surface level, it is only the most basic definition and does not fully address its deeper aspects and concepts. The full understanding of kamae includes the concepts of *uko* and *muko,* which respectively mean "kamae" and "no kamae." This is very important. The Eishin-ryu batto-ho uses five basic kamae with additional variations. These basic kamae include *jodan no kamae, chudan no kamae, gedan no kamae, in no kamae* and *yo no kamae.* Other styles utilize these kamae as well or variations of them. Additionally, some styles may have different kamae. All of these kamae are examples of uko, which are the structure and components or the "hard" aspects of kamae.

Proper kamae includes both outer *(omote)* and inner *(ura)* aspects referred to as *katachi* and *kokoro no kamae* (spirit of the form). Katachi represents the outer physical structure of kamae, including position and posture. Kokoro no kamae is the "inner kamae" and refers to those aspects of kamae that cannot be seen. An illustration of the principles of kamae can be seen in the construction and fortification of castles in feudal Japan. For example, the physical structures of the castle, such as its walls, and other defensive elements, perhaps a moat, represent the katachi (form) of the kamae of the castle. Kokoro no kamae is represented by that which is found inside the castle, such as the samurai and the daimyo. These are considered to be the kokoro no kamae of the castle because they cannot be seen from the outside. These elements all come together to form the kamae of the castle.

The example presented above should help clarify that proper kamae, whether that of an individual or of a castle, includes both katachi and kokoro no kamae. However, this is also uko, or the expression of kamae. You need to also understand muko as it relates to kamae in order to completely understand the dynamics of kamae. Muko refers to the nonexistence of a single kamae. Simply put, muko is "no kamae" because kamae is not simply for defense, like blocking an attack. Kamae is how to attack and is directly related to the position and movement of an opponent. Consider the image of two swordsmen facing each other; one assumes a chudan no kamae. If his opponent moves back, it causes the first swordsman to move naturally from chudan no kamae through *seigan no kamae* to jodan no kamae. The movement of the opponent dictated the first swordsman's change in kamae. The change in kamae as a result of an opponent's movement is the same concept as found in batto, in which the sword is drawn and cuts in response to the enemy's decision to attack. This change in kamae may continue until a *suki* (an opening) is detected. The effect of this natural changing of kamae results in muko, having "no kamae." In reality there are true physical kamae, but as a result of natural constant change, there is no set kamae. So, there is kamae but no kamae. This is uko-muko.

One final consideration concerning kamae is that kamae should exist "before kamae," meaning before the physical structure of kamae is set. This should be understood as being preparatory in nature and as such is connected to zanshin. Zanshin, remaining mind, refers to an awareness of and connection to your surroundings and opponents, real or potential, and should dictate preparatory positioning before the materialization of an opponent or an attack. This results in never being off-guard and having no suki. In short, zanshin is kamae. Without zanshin, there can be no kamae.

Chudan no kamae is the fundamental posture in Japanese sword arts. Sometimes referred to as *mizu no kamae* or *tsune no kamae*, its main characteristic is to control the centerline between two combatants. This position is the most effective for delivering a thrusting technique to the centerline of the opponent's body. Chudan no kamae allows the sword to block upward if necessary while performing the furikaburi. It is the fundamental posture for establishing control of the centerline in combat.

CHUDAN NO KAMAE (MIDDLE ATTITUDE)

1-2: Assume a natural position with the right foot forward and the body slightly turned toward the left. The *kissaki* is at throat height and the *tsuka gashira* should be level with the lower abdomen. The left hand is approximately four to five inches forward of the body. Pressure is pushed forward through the hips into the kissaki. This pressure is maintained in the kissaki by stretching the *tsuka* with both hands as the hips attempt to rotate and exert pressure forward and backward.

Jodan no kamae is a kamae that should be taken by those with confidence in their technical and spiritual strength. Its main characteristic is to exert cutting pressure on your opponent and control the combative space with your strong desire to win. Jodan no kamae is sometimes known as *hi no kamae,* referring to the fiery attitude that is elicited. This position should elicit a very aggressive attitude. This position is the most effective for delivering a kirioroshi or *kesa-giri* technique to the head or shoulders of the opponent's body.

JODAN NO KAMAE (UPPER ATTITUDE)

1-3: Assume a natural position with the left foot forward and the body slightly turned toward the right. The sword is held above the head with the *kissaki* pointing back at a 45-degree angle. The *tsuka gashira* should be in line with or slightly forward of the left elbow and the right hand in line with the front of the head. Pressure is pushed upward through the hips into the kissaki.

Gedan no kamae is another fundamental posture. Its main characteristic is to exert cutting pressure to the outside and centerline while maintaining a defensive nature. The kissaki is always ready to thrust or cut and the center and *koshi* of the blade defend the centerline from an oncoming attack. Gedan no kamae is sometimes referred to as *chi no kamae* or the earth position. From *gedan*, the sword can only move in one direction for defense or attack. This position should elicit an aggressive attitude and still conceal its defensive properties. This position is the most effective for delivering a *tsuki* to the leg or centerline or a *kiriage* across the opponent's wrists or body.

GEDAN NO KAMAE (LOWER ATTITUDE)

1-2: Assume a natural position with the right foot forward and the body slightly turned toward the left. The sword is held forward of the body with the *kissaki* pointing downward and in line with the outside of the right knee. The *tsuka gashira* should be in line with the left hip and the *tsuba* should be in line with the center of the body. Pressure is pushed forward through the hips into the kissaki.

Waki no kamae is an intermediate posture in the Japanese sword arts. Its main characteristic is to conceal the sword's cutting distance and pressure. Waki no kamae is sometimes referred to as yo no kamae. Yo no kamae expresses the attitude of things unseen—the ura. This position should elicit an aggressive and inviting attitude. Presenting the left should to the attacker limits his target areas and allows you to more accurately predict his next attack. This position is the most effective for hiding your own kiriage, *suihei, kesa* or kirioroshi technique.

WAKI NO KAMAE (SIDE ATTITUDE)

1-3: Assume a natural position with the left foot forward and the body turned fully toward the right. The sword is held to the side of the body with the *kissaki* pointing to the rear and downward in line with the outside of the right knee. The cutting edge should be turned slightly forward and downward. The *tsuka* is in line with the center of the body at the abdomen. Pressure is maintained in the kissaki by stretching the tsuka with the hips and hands.

Migi hasso no kamae or in no kamae is an intermediate posture in Japanese swords arts. It is also sometimes referred to as ki no kamae because the posture resembles a tree. Its main characteristic is to assess the cutting distance while facing right, which is the most natural position for a right-handed swordsman. Migi hasso no kamae presents the left shoulder to the enemy as the only open target area. By assuming this kamae, you are able to move freely through a crowded area and hold the sword in a ready position for longer periods of time. From this posture, it is easy to deliver a kesa-giri, kirioroshi or carry out an evasive maneuver. This position should elicit a calm and reflective attitude that allows the swordsman to quickly become offensive or defensive.

MIGI HASSO NO KAMAE (HIGH RIGHT-SIDE ATTITUDE)

1-3: Assume a natural position with the left foot forward with the body slightly turned toward the right. In *migi hasso no kamae*, the sword is held to the right side of the head with the *kissaki* pointing upward to the rear at a 45-degree angle. The *tsuba* should be held at face height: approximately one-fist distance from the right side of the face, and in line with the corner of the mouth. The cutting edge should be turned directly forward toward the opponent. The *tsuka gashira* is forward of the left elbow. Pressure is maintained in the kissaki by pushing upward thought the hips.

Hidari hasso no kamae, or yo no kamae, is also an intermediate posture. Its main characteristic is to assess the cutting distance while facing left and preparing for an angular attack. From hidari hasso no kamae, it is easy to deliver a left-to-right kesa-giri or transition into a left-to-right kiriage. This position should also elicit a calm and reflective attitude that allows the swordsman to quickly become offensive or defensive.

HIDARI HASSO NO KAMAE (HIGH LEFT-SIDE ATTITUDE)

1-3: Assume a natural position with the right foot forward and the body slightly turned toward the left. In *hidari hasso no kamae,* **the sword is held to the left side of the head with the** *kissaki* **pointing upward to the rear at a 45-degree angle. The** *tsuba* **should be held at face height: approximately one-fist distance from the left side of the face, and in line with the corner of the mouth. The cutting edge should be turned directly forward toward the opponent. The** *tsuka gashira* **is forward of the right elbow, and pressure is maintained in the kissaki by pushing upward though the hips.**

Jodan no kasumi is an advanced posture. Its main characteristic is to pressure the cutting distance while facing right and to prepare for an overhead attack. From jodan no kasumi, it is easy to deliver a right-to-left kesa-giri or kirioroshi. Transitioning into a left or right upward block or to jodan no kamae is also easily accomplished from this position. This kamae is very aggressive and allows the swordsman to quickly become offensive or defensive.

JODAN NO KASUMI (HIGH-LEVEL CONCEALED ATTITUDE)

1-3: Assume a natural position with the left foot forward and the body turned fully toward the right. In *jodan no kasumi,* the sword is held above the head to the right with the *kissaki* pointing forward on the centerline at a slight downward angle. The cutting edge should be turned upward. The *tsuba* should be held forward and slightly above the head. The right forearm is approximately the distance of one fist from the right side of the head, and the left wrist crosses in front of the right arm. The *tsuka gashira* is forward of the right elbow, and pressure is maintained in the kissaki by pushing forward though the hips.

Chudan no kasumi is an advanced posture. Its main characteristic is to pressure the centerline at close distance while facing right. It prepares the swordsman for a downward or angular attack. From chudan no kasumi, it is easy to deliver a thrust or perform an angular blocking technique. Transitioning into a left or right block or to chudan no kamae is also easily accomplished from this position. This kamae is very aggressive and allows the swordsman to quickly transition between offense or defense.

CHUDAN NO KASUMI (MID-LEVEL CONCEALED ATTITUDE)

1-3: Assume a natural position with the left foot forward and the body turned halfway toward the right. In *chudan no kasumi,* the sword is held in front of the body to the right with the *kissaki* pointing forward on the centerline at throat level. The cutting edge should be turned outward to the right side. The *tsuba* should be held forward and slightly above the left forearm. The right forearm is crossed over the left wrist. The *tsuka gashira* is forward of the right elbow, and pressure is maintained in the kissaki by pushing forward though the hips.

Gedan no kasumi is an advanced posture. Its main characteristic is to pressure the centerline at a close distance while facing right. It prepares the swordsman for a downward or frontal thrusting attack. From gedan no kasumi, it is easy to deliver a tsuki or horizontal attacking technique. Transitioning into a left or right block or to chudan no kamae is also easily accomplished from this position. This kamae is less aggressive than chudan no kasumi but allows the swordsman to quickly switch to an offensive or defensive movement.

GEDAN NO KASUMI (LOWER-LEVEL CONCEALED ATTITUDE)

1-3: Assume a natural position with the left foot forward and the body turned halfway toward the right. In *gedan no kasumi*, the sword is held in front of the body to the right with the *kissaki* pointing forward on the centerline at waist level. The cutting edge should be turned outward to the right side. The *tsuba* should be held forward and slightly above the left forearm. The right forearm is crossed over the left wrist. The *tsuka gashira* is forward of the right elbow, and pressure is maintained in the kissaki by pushing forward though the hips.

TE NO UCHI (CUTTING TECHNIQUE)

The *katana* evolved as an instrument meant for slicing and thrusting. The swords curvature allows a single point of the cutting edge to travel across the target as it cuts. This point of contact is supported by the back of the blade or *mune*. The energy is transferred through the mune directly to the cutting edge when the sword is swung in an elliptical curve. The combination of the curvature of the blade and the arc of the swing push the energy forward along the *monouchi* (cutting section of the blade) toward the kissaki. This transfer of energy is supported by the palms of the hands and the successive tightening of the grip, known as *tsuka no nigiri kata*. This gripping action is critical to keeping the edge traveling in a straight line. The line that the cutting edge travels along is known as the *hasuji otosu*. For the hasuji to be straight and true, the mune must be aligned directly behind the cutting edge in order for the transfer of power to remain effective. If there is an imbalance of power or support of the hands during the cut, the sword will cant at an angle or wiggle during the cut. This will end all transfer of energy to the cutting edge and transfer the energy to the lateral side of the blade.

TRAJECTORY OF THE OVERHEAD SWING

1-3: The sword describes an ellipse that passes overhead on its way to the target. The furthest point forward in the arc transfers the greatest energy to the edge of the blade.

In addition to proper alignment, the hands play a pivotal role in establishing *enshin-ryoku* (centripetal force). During a cut, the motions of the arms describe an elliptical sphere as the sword passes around the body in an infinite number of planes. Speed of the sword is increased by the extension of the arms, which creates a larger ellipse. This extension of the swing places the tip of the sword at a greater distance from the pivotal axis of the swing, thus increasing the overall speed of the cut. The gripping power of the hands, as they tighten around the tsuka during the cut, increases the speed of the kissaki by establishing a secondary axis from which the sword is allowed to pivot. The greatest speed is achieved at the furthest forward point on the ellipse causing centripetal force to multiply the cutting energy. This forward point should be centered just above or to the outside of the targeted area. As the contact point on the sword moves back toward the swordsman having already cut through its target, the energy of the sword continues to push forward along the cutting edge until the kissaki releases the final spent energy. The sword's energy is delivered to the target in the form of a slicing action.

The placement of the hand should remain consistent for cutting. The palms of the hands should be placed directly behind the tsuka. The bones at the inside of the wrists should lie on a straight line with the back of the tsuka and intersect each other on the same plane. The thumbs of both hands should be directly to the sides of the tsuka pointed in the same direction as the cutting edge.

TSUKA NO NIGIRI KATA—TWO-HAND GRIP

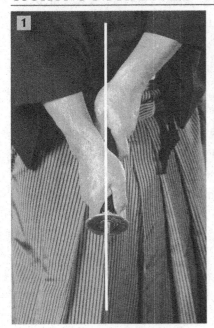 

1: Correct alignment of the wrists: Do not allow the wrists to rotate outward while holding the sword. If the thumbs approach the back of the *tsuka*, the hands cannot support the technique.

2: Incorrect alignment of the hands and wrists: The knuckles of the hands should align with the diamonds that are formed by the wrapping on the tsuka. One finger's distance should be maintained between the tsuba and the right hand. The distance between the hands is approximately two inches for fast cutting, but the hands transition farther apart to facilitate blocking and parrying. The left hand forces hip energy into the sword while the right hand generally adjusts the technical control. Pressure exerted by the grip is firm but relaxed. Start by squeezing with the little and ring fingers. As the grip tightens, continue to squeeze consecutively with the middle fingers and then lightly with the index fingers. The distance between the *tsuka gashira* and the right wrist is approximately the width of a single clenched fist.

CONTINUED ON NEXT PAGE

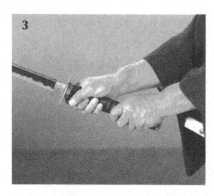  

3: Correct position of hands: Common mistakes found in the *te no uchi* of novices stem from overpowering or over-relaxing the grip tension. If the tension is too light, the wrists will turn outward and allow the thumbs to migrate above the tsuka.

4: Incorrect grip: Thumbs are rotated above the tsuka because of relaxed wrists. If the grip is too tight, as caused by excessively squeezing with the index fingers, energy is transferred away from the cutting edge toward the *mune*. Excessive gripping pulls the *kissaki* upward and expands the space between the right wrist and the tsuka gashira.

5: Incorrect grip: The sword is pulled back by excessive gripping power in the index fingers.

During nukitsuke, the right hand is required to control the direction, power and placement of the cutting stroke. It is in this technique that battojutsu is defined. *Te no uchi* determines the success or failure of nukitsuke. Because nukitsuke is a dynamic transition from very little to a complete grip, te no uchi changes throughout the cutting process. It is a consecutive, evolutionary process of squeezing the fingers and exerting the tension of the right hand across the tsuka. The squeezing process is also a procedure of incrementally increasing the speed at which the fingers close while the technique unfolds. The use of the left hand to control the saya and "feed" the tsuka into the right hand becomes a study in itself.

The finish position for the cut with the right hand is identical to that of a two-hand grip. The palm is placed directly behind and supports the back of the tsuka. The right hand is one inch from the tsuba. The distance between the *tsuka gashira* and the right forearm should be no more or less than the distance of one fist. When performing a horizontal nukitsuke, the knuckles of the right hand on the tsuka form a likeness to Mount Fuji when viewed from the front.

TSUKA NO NIGIRI KATA—ONE-HAND GRIP

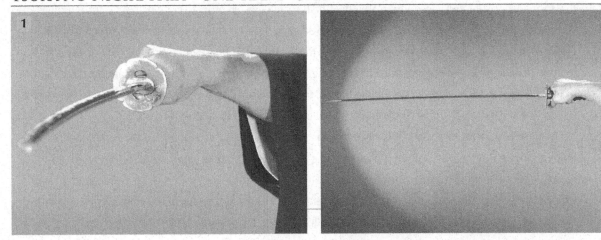

1: Correct grip: A common mistake is to turn the right wrist upward while reaching for or exerting pressure on the *tsuka*. In this position, the back of the hand is parallel to the wrist. The palm will no longer support the pressure against the cutting edge, and the power of the cut is not transferred through the *mune* to the cutting edge.

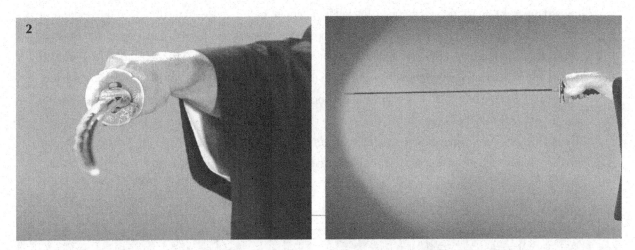

2: Incorrect grip: Here the wrist and hand have rotated upward and placed the thumb knuckle behind the tsuka.

NUKITSUKE—SHALLOW-DRAWING CUT

The defining technique in the curriculum of battojutsu was developed as a method of surprising the enemy by attacking unexpectedly while the sword was still in the saya. The founder of the art was inspired to defeat his enemy by drawing the sword and cutting through his adversary in a single uninterrupted motion. This very first movement, in which life and death hung in the balance, changed the Japanese sword arts forever. To draw the sword is referred to as batto. Thus was born the art of battojutsu.

Although battojutsu refers to drawing a sword from the saya, it does not necessarily imply a cutting action. The sword can be drawn from the saya into a kamae, and this motion is still considered batto. In actuality, it is called nukitsuke when the drawing action is used to cut in a singular motion and when the kissaki leaves the saya. Nukitsuke implies a sudden attack that originates from the saya.

Nukitsuke has evolved since the time of Hayashizaki Jinsuke Shigenobu. Many variations of the technique were developed by a succession of masters that have followed the tradition. The changing circumstances that samurai encountered gave birth to abundant *heiho* (strategies) in order to cope with their surroundings. Numerous methods of nukitsuke were developed to adapt to these changing environments. All of the original methods of drawing and cutting remain. In addition to the original techniques, other manifestations exist that include drawing to countless angles and employing blocking and parrying techniques that flow directly in to cut the enemy. The variations are limitless. Thus, to perform nukitsuke correctly, what is needed is years of practice and guidance under the watchful eye of an experienced instructor.

Nukitsuke starts from a preparatory standing or walking position, depending on the technique that is being employed. Because a standing posture is the fundamental starting point for all Eishin-ryu batto-ho waza, this position will be used in the book's descriptions of nukitsuke. For the purpose of delineating several specific methods of drawing and cutting, we will refer to nukitsuke as drawing and cutting specifically with the kissaki. This is a shallow cut that should be followed by a more severe strike to the body utilizing the monouchi. Each principle aspect of nukitsuke is a study unto itself. Continual examination and refinement of the smallest details is necessary if you intend to truly understand the subtle intricacies of the technique.

Nukitsuke starts from a fully sheathed position. While standing, move both hands simultaneously toward the tsuka. In shoden techniques, the left hand encircles the saya with the thumb at the uppermost part on the tsuba. This action occurs slightly before the right hand touches the tsuka. Special care must be exercised to ensure that the left thumb is off of the direct line of the saya to the inside as it is placed on the tsuba. Just as the right hand begins to grasp the tsuka, the left thumb presses almost imperceptibly forward against the edge of the tsuba, pushing it about one-half inch forward. Because the *habaki* usually fits quite snugly into the koiguchi, this loosens the sword from the saya to ensure a smooth and fast draw. This subtle yet essential movement is called *koiguchi no kiri kata* (cutting the fish mouth). And the particular method that is used in shoden-level waza is referred to as *soto-giri* (outside cutting) koiguchi no kiri kata.

KOIGUCHI NO KIRI KATA

1: Push the *tsuba* forward with the left thumb.

2: The left hand performs *koiguchi no kiri kata*.

In addition to this basic method of koiguchi no kiri kata, there are two variations. One alternative is to keep the tip of the thumb hidden behind the tsuba. The thumb then pushes against the back of the tsuba rather than pushing against the top edge. This hides the movement from the opponent and may delay his reaction a few tenths of a second. This variation is called *uchi-giri* (inside cutting) and is the preferred method used in Eishin-ryu batto-ho.

There is another variation that does not use the thumb at all. With the left hand wrapped around the saya and very close to the tsuba, the hand squeezes against the saya. This action broadens the width of the hand and forces the tsuba forward as it expands. This variation is employed when you are uncertain of your opponent's intentions but you want a possible advantage should the need arise. With this variation, the opening of the koiguchi goes completely unnoticed while the right hand remains relaxed and unthreatening.

"Drawing the sword" is truly a poor explanation of what is actually happening during the process of nukitsuke. To "draw the sword" supposes a pulling action. The actual feeling should be that of "pushing away" the enemy while your right hand rises up the centerline of attack. This pushing motion is accomplished by turning the body to the left and extending an already straightened arm forward and up. Any pulling action that originates from the right elbow can be easily thwarted by the enemy's oncoming charge. It is also disconnected from the hip rotation that gives *nukitsuke* its power. A committed pushing action will continue to pressure the opponent at every stage of the draw.

GRASPING THE SWORD

1: Just as *koiguchi no kiri kata* is completed, the right hand grasps the tsuka calmly with the fingers touching near the middle knuckles.

2: The fingers and thumb should lightly grasp the sword while the left and right arm push forward and down as they straighten.

3: Turn to the left to allow the sword to threaten the centerline and seize control of the combative space between you and the enemy.

CONTINUED ON NEXT PAGE

4: Release the *kissaki* from the *saya*. Step forward and expand the chest by contracting the back muscles as you pull the shoulder blades together. At the same time, allow the kissaki to be released from the saya and follow your right arm across the line of attack.

5: Expand the chest and cut. Proper *tsuka no nigiri kata* with your right hand will add centripetal force to the cut. These actions should not feel disjointed or separate. The cutting action should be smooth and accelerate from the beginning to the end of the movement. *Nukitsuke* becomes a function of the entire frontal side of the body, expanding toward the enemy while the sword is attached to this expansion. The expansion of the chest is complimented by hip rotation that adds to the power of the cut.

The process of koiguchi no kiri kata and drawing the sword up to the kissaki is identical for all nukitsuke. However at the moment of saya banare (separating from the saya), the hips may rotate clockwise or counterclockwise. Either direction will increase the wounding power of the cut. The decision to use either method is dependent on which tactic is considered the most prudent follow-up technique to destroy the enemy's defenses. Two methods of hip rotation have traditionally been used in Eishin-ryu. They are the *Shimomura-ha* and the *Tanimura-ha* methods of nukitsuke.

The method of hip rotation that was passed down through the Shimomura branch of Eishin-ryu is defensive in nature. The left hip pulls back and rotates counterclockwise at the moment of saya banare. The heel of the rear foot is forced downward to support the forward motion of the right hip. This movement puts full pressure in the kissaki at the end of the nukitsuke. The left hip supports the kissaki in its ability to thrust sharply forward at the end of the drawing cut. Power in the very tip of the kissaki requires the hips to continue to rotate counterclockwise to maintain pressure against the enemy's possible counterattack. It is for this reason that this version of nukitsuke is considered defensive in nature. This hip rotation is found in most of the shoden waza of Eishin-ryu batto-ho. Shimomura-ha nukitsuke is a faster method of drawing the sword when the body is changing directions from right to left as in the waza known as *koteki gyakuto.*

SHIMOMURA-HA NUKITSUKE

1: Position the sword to begin *Shimomura saya banare*.

2: Begin a counterclockwise hip rotation.

3: Finish with the left hip pulled back and heel pushed down.

The advantage of Shimomura-ha nukitsuke is in its ability to support a powerful thrust with the kissaki. But the solidity of the hips in this position limits the mobility of the swordsman to move quickly forward at a great distance if the need arises. The left foot is firmly rooted to the ground and the left hip is pulled back to support the right hips forward projection. In order to move forward quickly with the left foot, the corresponding left hip must be released from its counterclockwise rotation. This change in direction may consume the critical time that is necessary to seize on a weakness in the opponent's defenses if he is moving away from you. The Eishin-ryu batto-ho curriculum offers a solution to an enemy who is moving away rather than pressuring your centerline of attack. The Tanimura-ha nukitsuke addresses this scenario.

The method of hip rotation that was passed down through the Tanimura branch of Eishin-ryu is slightly "more" offensive in nature. The left hip rotates clockwise at the moment of saya banare. The heel of the rear foot is allowed to support the forward motion of the left hip. This movement puts full pressure in the monouchi during the cut. The left foot and hip are free to continue to move forward quickly and pursue an opponent that is moving away. This hip rotation is found in the Eishin-ryu batto-ho okuden waza known as *zenteki gyakuto sono ichi*. Although the right hip supports the kissaki in its ability to thrust forward at the end of the drawing cut, the left hip must be rotated counterclockwise to facilitate a thrust. Tanimura-ha nukitsuke is a faster method of drawing the sword when changing body direction from left to right as in the waza known as *koteki nukiuchi*.

TANIMURA-HA NUKITSUKE

1: Position the sword for *Tanimura saya banare.*

2: Perform a clockwise hip rotation.

3: The left hip should finish in line with right hip at the end of *nukitsuke.*

Each of these methods of hip rotation presents the Eishin-ryu swordsman an opportunity to adjust to his changing environment.

Nukitsuke must be studied in-depth to understand its limitless potential. Even though a waza may stipulate nukitsuke is to be delivered in a predetermined direction, each nukitsuke represents all of the various angles that may address open targets or changing circumstances. Practicing the variations of nukitsuke becomes a study in recognizing the opening and closing of target areas and the ability to maintain *yoyu* (a margin for change) in your technique. The left hand is responsible for adapting to the target area that is presented by the enemy. The right hand is responsible for the pressuring the centerline of attack.

Each angle of attack and the cutting distance to the target area evolves and changes because the spatial relationship between the combatants is dynamic. The various angles and methods of employing nukitsuke address the dynamic nature of these combative environments.

SUIHEI—HORIZONTAL CUT

1: As the *kissaki* is preparing to separate from the *saya*, turn the *mune* of the blade inward toward your body. Rotate the sword into the right hand. This action feeds the *tsuka* into the proper position in the hand.

2: As the right hand begins to contract around the tsuka, continue to turn the torso toward the left. This action allows the *tsuka gashira* to maintain constant pressure on the centerline as the sword is drawn to a greater length.

3: Before the kissaki leaves the saya, allow the tsuka gashira to move left and create a wider angle to the target from your left side. Open the left hip and shoulder to release the kissaki. Rotate the right hand to allow the kissaki to travel along a horizontal plane across the top of the chest.

4: As the *monouchi* leads the sword across the centerline, continue to expand the chest and extend the energy toward the kissaki. The top knuckles of the right hand should travel across the body at the height of the right shoulder. The kissaki should travel along its cutting plane at the bottom of the *tsuba*. The finish position should place the tsuka gashira pointing directly behind you at approximately one fist's distance from your right forearm. The kissaki extends forward at the height of the bottom of the tsuba.

The second possible angle of attack during nukitsuke allows the sword to cut diagonally upward in kiriage. Kiriage is used to cut with the kissaki to the body or the wrists. The cutting plane of kiriage (a rising cut) covers the entire vertical position of the opponent's body. As the sword leaves the saya, it retains the potential to cut the extremities with the monouchi or the body with the kissaki. Crucial to the success of kiriage is to limit the movement of the right hip throughout the cut. Should the right hip retract at any time while the blade is in contact with the target, it will cease its cutting action. The kissaki must continue to move forward to the farthest distance from your right shoulder.

KIRIAGE—RISING CUT

1: When the *habaki* is preparing to separate from the *saya*, turn the *mune* of the blade dramatically inward toward your body. This action feeds the *tsuka* into the proper position in the right hand.

2: As the right hand begins to contract around the tsuka, push the saya downward and continue to turn the torso toward the left. This action allows the *tsuka gashira* to maintain constant pressure on the centerline as the sword is drawn to a greater length.

3: Prior to the kissaki leaving the saya, allow the tsuka gashira to create a wider angle to the target from your left side. Open the left hip and shoulder to release the kissaki. Rotate the right hand to allow the kissaki to travel upward along a diagonal plane across the torso.

CONTINUED ON NEXT PAGE

4: As the *monouchi* leads the sword across the centerline, continue to expand the chest and extend the energy toward the kissaki. The kissaki should travel on a diagonal plane upward across the enemy from the lower right hip through his left shoulder.

5: The finish position should place the tsuka gashira facing directly behind you approximately one fist's distance from your right forearm. The kissaki points forward at the height of the bottom of the *tsuba*. Finish the cut with power in the kissaki.

The third angle of attack allows the sword to travel diagonally downward during its cutting action. This kesa-giri is used to cut with the kissaki to the face or body. The cutting plane of kesa-giri (downward angular cut) covers the entire vertical position of the opponent's body or face. As the sword leaves the saya, it retains the potential to cut the extremities with the monouchi or the body with the kissaki. The success of kesa-giri is in the movement and expansion of the hips and chest throughout the cut. The monouchi must continue to lead the kissaki downward as it cuts. Care must be taken to avoid pointing with the kissaki while cutting. Maintain one fist's distance between the tsuka gashira and the right forearm throughout the cutting action.

KESA-GIRI—DOWNWARD ANGULAR CUT

1: As the *kissaki* is preparing to separate from the *saya*, turn the *mune* of the blade slightly inward toward your body. This action feeds the *tsuka* into the proper position in the hand.

2: As the right hand begins to contract around the tsuka, push the sword forward and continue to turn the torso toward the left. This action allows the *tsuka gashira* to maintain constant pressure on the centerline as the sword is drawn to a greater length.

3: Before the kissaki leaves the saya, allow the tsuka gashira to rise slightly to create a wider angle to the target from your left side. Open the left hip and shoulder to release the kissaki. Rotate the right hand to allow the kissaki to travel along a diagonal downward plane across the face or chest.

4: As the *monouchi* leads the cut across the centerline, continue to expand the chest and extend the energy toward the kissaki. The kissaki should travel on a diagonal plane downward from the upper right shoulder through the opponent's left lower rib.

5: The finish position should place the tsuka gashira facing directly forward of your right hip. Maintain approximately one fist's distance between your right forearm and the tsuka gashira. The kissaki points forward at the height of the lowest rib. Finish the cut with a powerful connection to your right hip.

NUKIUCHI—DEEP-DRAWING CUT

Nukiuchi starts in a manner identical to nukitsuke. Nukiuchi implies a sudden strike to a targeted area of the opponent. In this book, we will refer to nukiuchi as drawing and cutting specifically with the monouchi. This attack should be delivered to targets that are less resistant to the power applied by a one-hand cut. The target areas attacked by using a nukiuchi include the neck, wrists, face, armpits and leg areas. Practitioners refrain from attacking the body with the monouchi while only using one hand out of fear of having the blade become trapped. The crucial time that is necessary to withdraw a stuck sword from a body during a confrontation can mean the difference between life and death to the swordsman. It is for this reason that a complete study of target areas and the effect that a sword may have on them should be undertaken.

When performing nukiuchi it must be remembered that the targeted area of the opponent is closer to you than when you are performing nukitsuke. Specifically, it is closer by the length of distance that exists between the monouchi and kissaki of your own sword. In single combat with swords, this would be the equivalent to the difference in combative ranges between using artillery vs. ground troops. Although in this case, it would be the ground troops that impose the most damage on the enemy at close quarters. The monouchi cuts deeply and for that reason it retains the ability to inflict greater harm. The deeper the cut the greater it incapacitates the enemy.

The preparation and action leading up to the cut are done exactly as described for nukitsuke. These pictures present a number of target areas that are specific to nukiuchi.

SUIHEI—DEEP HORIZONTAL CUT

1: To stop an opponent's *nukitsuke*, cut *suihei* with the *monouchi* to his right upper arm. As the monouchi leads the sword across the centerline, continue to fully expand the chest and extend the energy toward the *kissaki*. Develop the power that is generated by turning the hips to effectively cut through his arm.

KIRIAGE—DEEP RISING CUT

1: To stop an opponent's *nukitsuke* when it is in the initial stages, cut *kiriage* with the *monouchi* to his right hand or wrist. Cut upward with a deep kiriage to sever the wrist and hand. Develop the power to cut fully through the extremities to the center-line of the body.

KESA-GIRI—DOWNWARD ANGULAR CUT

1: To severely injure an opponent to your front or right corner, cut *kesa-giri* toward the neck if it is exposed.

2: Cut to the wrists if they are protecting the head while in *jodan* or *hasso*. The downward stroke must be strong enough to penetrate deeply. Develop the power to cut fully through the extremities to the centerline of the body.

To severely injure an opponent, learn to cut simultaneously with both the kissaki and the monouchi. All cuts should be delivered as though the monouchi is cutting the target first. It is the leading edge when the sword crosses the centerline of the cutting axis. It is therefore the first part of the sword to defend the battleground during the drawing of the sword. The kissaki follows the monouchi into battle and continues to cut as both travel along the same cutting plane. In the case of *nito* (two swords) for nukiuchi or nukitsuke, the monouchi is looked on as the long sword and the kissaki is used as the short sword. Wielding the sword in this manner makes it possible to cut the enemy by using two separate cutting surfaces simultaneously.

NITO—TWO SWORDS

1: As the enemy approaches in *jodan no kamae*, cut directly to his face with the kissaki as you cut through his wrist with the monouchi. There are many opportunities to use both the kissaki and the monouchi to simultaneously cut the enemy.

FURIKABURI—RAISING THE SWORD

The transitional movements that take place between what appears to be the cutting actions in battojutsu contain the quintessence of spiritual intent. Quite often close examination of what appears to be an inconsequential transitional movement unveils the face of mastery. This is particularly true of the movements that connect the cutting techniques of nukitsuke and kirioroshi. One of these significant transitions can be found between the drawing stroke of nukitsuke and the beginning of the finishing stroke of kirioroshi (downward cut). This transitional movement is known as *furikaburi*.

Furikaburi is the process of lifting the sword to execute a downward cut. But it is much more than that to a trained swordsman. It is an opportunity to attack if there is an opening in the opponent's defenses while he is lifting his sword to cut. It is the continuation of a thrusting action initiated immediately following the nukitsuke or it may be a threatening gesture to forestall an opponent's ability to cut. Furikaburi may transition into a blocking action performed as the sword is raised in preparation for a downward cut or it can be a deflection of the opponent's blade when he cuts to your head as you move. Correct performance of furikaburi is one of the hallmarks of an expert swordsman if it is performed with all of the potential, inherent applications.

The technical explanation of the technique does not capture the pressure and intent that is necessary to perform it correctly. Kihaku (energized motion) must be present to keep the sword alive in the hand. And the most important aspect of furikaburi, the mark of an expert swordsman, is the ability to hold and cut the adversary at every single moment. At the end of a horizontal nukitsuke or nukiuchi, the pressure to attack should be evident in the kissaki. As you move forward to overtake the enemy, the kissaki pressures into the center of the combative space to control the attacker. This action attempts to control the enemy's *kuzushi* (balance) and *sei-chu-sen* (centerline). However, it does not always prevent the opponent from moving away from the pressure in order to reestablish his balance and launch an attack. The following methods of furikaburi offer countermeasures in order to control, deflect or sweep aside an oncoming attack if it occurs during the raising of the sword for a finishing cut.

The most common method of performing furikaburi is to allow the sword to move along a horizontal plane as the kissaki, *hoshi* and then monouchi continue to pressure the opponent. This allows the kissaki to pass by the left ear and behind the back of the head while maintaining the ability to cut the enemy.

SUIHEI—HORIZONTAL

1: Maintain pressure in the *kissaki* at the end of *nukitsuke*. Continue to exert control over the enemy with the power of your forward momentum and hips.

2: Continue to move your body forward from the hips as you close the distance to the opponent. Allow this forward motion to project through the kissaki to the enemy. Begin to rotate your left shoulder and hip forward as you push the kissaki toward the centerline of attack.

CONTINUED ON NEXT PAGE

3: As the kissaki passes the centerline of attack, bend the wrist on the horizontal plane to begin to push the kissaki toward the left shoulder. The cutting energy moves back across the *hoshi* (angled sword tip) toward the *monouchi* as the sword passes the centerline. The sword retains the ability to cut throughout this movement by reopening the chest and hips as in nukitsuke.

4: When the *tsuba* has reached the centerline of the body, begin to bend the right elbow so that the kissaki moves over the left shoulder near the ear. At the same time, begin to turn the cutting edge of the blade upward as the left hand moves under the *tsuka* to take a two-hand grip.

5: As the kissaki is pushed back over the head, maintain power on the cutting edge of the blade. Do not allow the energy to drop through the sword to the *mune* when the kissaki drops below the level of the back of the head. Proper tsuka no nigiri kata will prevent the sword from "dying" in this position.

6: Begin the next cut by pushing the energy through the *monouchi* toward the kissaki. Extend the monouchi upward to begin the cut. This will be a natural continuation of *furikaburi* if the energy has remained present while the sword was pushed over the head and shoulders. Extend the arms as the hands move forward overhead.

7: Continue to extend the arms forward and up before making contact with the monouchi to the target area. Be certain to make a full extension of the arms following furikaburi and the initial stages of *kirioroshi*.

If you pressure the centerline with the kissaki and the opponent shifts to your left or attempts to cut your head before your right hand is on the centerline, then furikaburi is converted into a sweeping *(harai)* action to deflect the attacker's blade to the left and beyond your shoulder. The tsuka continues to move directly up the centerline and carries the kissaki behind the head to begin the kirioroshi to the enemy's head.

HARAI—SWEEPING

1: Maintain pressure in the *kissaki* at the end of *nukitsuke*. Continue to exert control over the enemy with the power of your forward momentum and hips.

2: Continue to move your body forward from the hips as you close the distance to the opponent. Allow this forward motion to project through the kissaki to the enemy. Begin to rotate your left shoulder and hip forward as you push the kissaki toward the centerline of attack.

CONTINUED ON NEXT PAGE

3: As the kissaki passes the centerline of attack, bend the wrist on the horizontal plane to begin to push the kissaki toward the left shoulder. The cutting energy moves back across the *hoshi* (angled sword tip) toward the *monouchi* as the sword passes the centerline. The sword retains the ability to cut throughout this movement by reopening the chest and hips as in nukitsuke.

4: Just before the *tsuba* has reached the centerline of the body, bend the right wrist while you push the palm of the right hand to the left. Push the *tsuka* up the centerline when the kissaki is pushed toward the outer point of the left shoulder. Raise the sword in a sweeping action. At the moment of contact with the opponent's blade, quickly turn your right wrist to flip the *shinogi* of the blade upward to intercept the enemy's sword near the *omote* (left side) middle section of your sword. This wrist action pushes the enemy's sword laterally to the left until the opponent's sword is parried past your own left shoulder.

5: Allow the kissaki to circle behind your head as the left hand moves under the tsuka to take a two-hand grip. As the kissaki is pushed back over the head, maintain power in the shinogi and cutting edge of the blade. Do not allow the energy to drop through the sword to the *mune* when the kissaki circles below the back of the head. Proper *tsuka no nigiri kata* will prevent the sword from "dying" in this position. Continue to cut by pushing the energy through the monouchi toward the kissaki. This will be a natural continuation of the circular *furikaburi* if the energy has remained present as the sword was pushed over the head and shoulders.

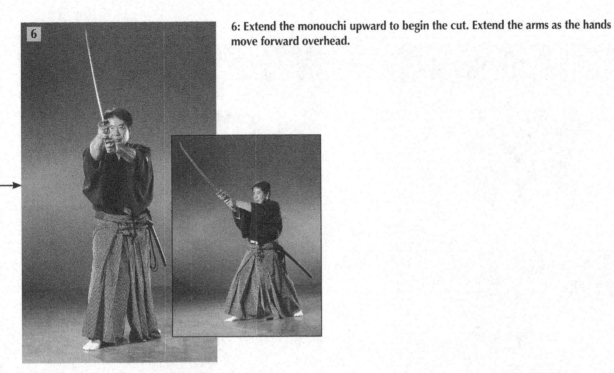

6: Extend the monouchi upward to begin the cut. Extend the arms as the hands move forward overhead.

If the opponent shifts to your right or attempts to cut to your head or right wrist from above, furikaburi is used to push up *(suriage)* and deflect the attacker's blade to the right beyond your shoulder. The tsuka continues to move directly up the centerline and carries the kissaki behind the head to begin the kirioroshi to the enemy's head.

SURIAGE—PUSHING UP

1: Maintain pressure in the *kissaki* at the end of *nukitsuke.* Continue to exert control over the enemy with the power of your forward momentum and hips.

2: Continue to move your body forward from the hips as you close the distance to the opponent. Allow this forward motion to project through the kissaki to the enemy. Begin to rotate your left shoulder and hip forward as you push the kissaki toward the centerline of attack.

3: As the kissaki passes the centerline of attack, begin to bend the wrist on the horizontal plane to push the kissaki toward the left shoulder. The cutting energy moves back across the *hoshi* (angled sword tip) toward the *monouchi* as the sword passes the centerline. Continue to move the kissaki toward the left ear. The sword retains the ability to cut throughout this movement by reopening the chest and hips like in nukitsuke.

4: Just before the *tsuba* has reached the centerline of the body, quickly rotate the right wrist clockwise in front of you to cause the monouchi to swing powerfully upward and to the right. Raise the sword while sweeping with the *shinogi*. Be sure to rotate the wrist powerfully to add centripetal force to the monouchi. Catch the opponent's blade with the monouchi on the *ura* (right side) of your sword. At the moment of contact with the opponent's blade, quickly turn your right wrist counterclockwise to allow the *ha* of the blade to flip the enemy's sword to the right.

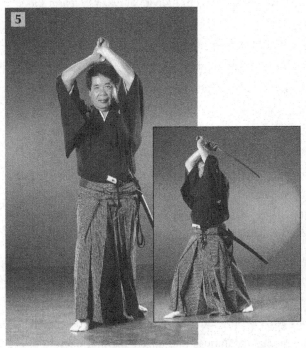

5: Continue to push the *tsuka* up the centerline as the kissaki is pushed upward over the head. As the kissaki is pushed back over the head, maintain power in the kissaki and cutting edge of the blade. Do not allow the energy to drop through the sword to the *mune* when the kissaki is pushed to the back of the head. Proper *tsuka no nigiri kata* will prevent the sword from "dying" in this position. Continue to cut by pushing the energy through the monouchi toward the kissaki.

6: Extend the arms when the hands move forward overhead. Extend the monouchi upward to begin the cut.

Kirioroshi—Downward Cut

There are few people who have not been impressed by the sound and the beauty of the long sword's arc and *tachi-kaze* (sword wind) when it whistles through the air. Tachi-kaze was often the last sound a samurai ever heard. It is most evident during kirioroshi—the powerful downward stroke of the samurai sword—that has captured the imagination of millions and brought death to many unfortunate individuals who have engaged it in real battles.

Mastering the technique of kirioroshi is the elusive study of doing less and less to achieve more and more. The Japanese katana is designed to slice when the cutting edge passes across its target. The concept appears to be simple, but in reality, the combination of factors necessary to generate the substantial cutting power to cleave through a large object takes years of study and consideration toward objective, strategic and psychological details.

The key to the successful practice of kirioroshi is to practice big movements. Big movements with the sword create enshin-ryoku—the centripetal force that is necessary to power a sword through an enemy's defenses or attacks. Large movements naturally cover greater distances. Control of the combative space is accomplished by the *kenshi,* whose sword cuts through it first. The bigger the movement and the greater the extension of the arms, the more rapidly the outcome can be achieved.

Since the time of Oe Masamichi, 17th grandmaster of Eishin-ryu, the curriculum has been taught in a tiered system. Before Oe Masamichi's revisions, there were hundreds of individual waza to learn. Oe categorized these techniques according to the importance they played in the evolution of the Eishin-ryu swordsman. He also assigned a method of teaching according to the attributes you would expect to find in a beginner, novice or advanced practitioner. He reduced the number of waza in the curriculum, then divided them into sets that were labeled as shoden (first transmission), chuden (middle transmission) and okuden (deep transmission).

Shoden techniques are taught as a method of establishing good habits and safe training practices. The practice of this type of movement establishes large technique and an understanding of combative space and timing. In most old schools of traditional budo, the first stages of learning involved mastering these very same principles of large combative spaces and the understanding of your range of movement. The kihon, waza, kumitachi and *suemonogiri* are taught precisely this way today at the shoden level.

Chuden techniques traditionally bring the practitioner into close contact with the enemy. As the budoka develops the understanding of space, timing and technical mastery of basics, his ability to respond faster and at closer ranges becomes a natural byproduct of the training. At this point, the introduction of waza and kihon that are reserved for just such environments are introduced to the swordsman.

Okuden level are the techniques of one who has gone deeply into the study of the kihon. It is the understanding of the depth and breadth of the fundamental techniques that makes the introduction of new variation possible. The technical variation at the okuden training is not a new method of performing a technique. It is an evolution of the student's understanding of the strengths and weaknesses in the movements as they transpire.

Kirioroshi begins with the sword raised overhead and prepared to deliver a final blow. The cut is delivered by putting power in the monouchi and extending the sword upward in an elliptical arc until it meets the head or shoulders of the opponent. The centripetal force is accelerated by performing the correct tsuka no nigiri kata in conjunction with *shibori* (wringing action) of the hands when you fully extend the arms. It is all done in a manner that the blade travels downward in a perfect hasuji through the target following the initial impact. Any waver or wiggle of the blade in an indication of improper te no uchi.

Shoden kirioroshi is taught to everyone and should be the mainstay of all practice. The purpose of practicing delivering the kirioroshi without changing the hip and shoulder position is to isolate the arm movement so as to not interrupt the natural downward swing of the arms. Any lateral motion by the body forces the blade to move sideways. Care should be taken to establish an unwavering hasuji and a swing that travels naturally back toward your center. Often, beginners swing the sword too hard or drop their elbows during the cut. This produces a chopping action and should be avoided. A clear indication of too much power or dropping of the elbows is a bounce that occurs at the bottom of the cut.

SHODEN KIRIOROSHI

1: The preparatory position for *kirioroshi* finds the *kissaki* pointing downward to the rear at a 45-degree angle. The *tsuka gashira* points upward to the front at 45 degrees.

2: Maintain tightness in the lower abdomen as you push gently upward into the hips to initiate the first movement. Put power in the *monouchi* and *kissaki* when you push the sword upward. Begin to extend the elbows in the direction of the sword. Extend the wrists and forearms upward while the sword travels forward above the head in a big arc.

CONTINUED ON NEXT PAGE

3: As the arms begin to lower from the highest point on the arc, squeeze the hands on the *tsuka* to propel the sword forward in a powerful forward cut. The impact point on the target occurs when the arms are at their greatest distance forward of the shoulders. The monouchi should achieve the height of the impact point at the top of the head when the arms are at full extension from the shoulders.

4: Allow the arms to swing naturally back toward the body as the tsuka gashira lowers toward your center. Do not allow the hips or shoulders to move while the blade draws downward through the centerline of attack. Finish with the monouchi of the sword parallel to the ground. The kissaki is at the same level as the bottom of the *tsuba*.

The purpose of *okuden kirioroshi* is to give the swordsman the additional cutting power of a longer blade and a deeper cut when the cutting edge passes through the target. Shorter swords were the result of edicts passed by the *shogun* during the Edo period in Japan. *Tachi,* which are long curved swords worn with armor, allowed the samura*i* to cut at a great distance from their enemy. The cutting edge and particularly the monouchi of the tachi were much longer than that of the katana. To compensate for the shorter sword's reach and lack of cutting power, the Eishin-ryu masters developed powerful extension of the arc in kirioroshi by opening the hips during the contact period of the cut. The beginning stages of okuden kiriorshi are identical to shoden kirioroshi. In fact, if any of the delivery of the sword in shoden kirioroshi is altered before the sword makes contact with the target area, the okuden kirioroshi will fail. The okuden techniques are pinnacles at the top of a great pyramid that are supported by the shoden techniques. They do not exist without a solid foundation in the kihon.

OKUDEN KIRIOROSHI

1: The preparatory position for *okuden kirioroshi* is the same as *shoden* with the *kissaki* pointing downward to the rear at a 45-degree angle. The *tsuka gashira* points upward to the front at 45 degrees.

2: Maintain tightness in the lower abdomen while you push gently upward into the hips to initiate the first movement. Put power in the *monouchi* and kissaki as you push the sword upward. Begin to extend the elbows in the direction of the sword. Extend the wrists and forearms upward when the sword travels forward above the head in a big arc. Continue to extend the power into the kissaki.

3: As the arms begin to lower from the highest point on the arc, squeeze the hands on the *tsuka* to propel the sword forward in a powerful forward cut. The impact point on the target occurs when the arms are at their greatest distance forward of the shoulders. The monouchi should achieve the height of the impact point at the top of the head when the arms are at full extension from the shoulders.

CONTINUED ON NEXT PAGE

4: As the monouchi makes contact with the target, begin to push both knees outward. The pressure should be felt on the outside edges of both feet.

5: Allow the arms to swing naturally back toward the body when the tsuka gashira lowers toward your center. Do not allow the hips or shoulders to move while the blade draws downward through the centerline of attack. Finish with the sword parallel to the ground and the body's weight over the center of the hips. The kissaki is at the same level as the bottom of the *tsuba*.

KIRITSUKE—SHALLOW CUT

Combat is dynamic. It is death-defying improvisation. The time it takes for a sword to pass through a five-inch target at optimum speed is 1/100,000 of a second. The margin for error in timing against an adversary is commensurate. If a kirioroshi fully misses its target in combat, the opportunity for recovery against a veteran swordsman is diminutive.

There are times when target opportunities that you are presented with may be less than lethal but still valuable in overcoming the enemy. Shallow cuts often open the door to opportunities for victory. Yoyu, the ability to change at any moment within the execution of technique, allows the swordsman's subconscious to recognize, evaluate and adapt to changing circumstances, even in that 1/100,000 of a second.

Kiritsuke is a cut that stops its trajectory immediately after it ceases cutting or misses its mark. It should finish with the *kissaki* somewhere along the centerline of the opponent's body. A kiritsuke can be instantly morphed into a block, parry or thrust. A shallow or failed cut must be immediately seen as an opportunity to control the centerline. If one fails to control the line of attack at this point, the opponent will seize on the moment and cut you down. Whereas kirioroshi begins with the kissaki low behind the head, kiritsuke usually begins to move from a kamae. The cutting action remains similar to kirioroshi. Always try to cut first with the monouchi. If the opponent begins to move away from you during the instant of intended impact, continue to follow through with the cut until the kissaki cuts or misses the intended target. Then stop! Protect the line of attack and seize the opportunity to thrust, cut forward or change cutting direction. Control the line of attack to prevent the enemy from filling the combative space.

KIRITSUKE

1: The preparatory position for *kiritsuke* can be *jodan, hasso, waki* or any other *kamae*. The *kissaki* and *monouchi* should be held with the feeling as though they already have the power to cut. The downward cut should always move through jodan when it cuts.

2: To begin the cut, shuffle forward with the front foot. Maintain tightness in the lower abdomen when you push upward through the hips to initiate the first movement. Put power in the monouchi and kissaki when you push the sword upward. Extend the elbows in the direction of the sword while you cut *kesa-giri*.

3: As the arms begin to lower from the highest point on the arc, squeeze the hands on the *tsuka* to propel the sword in a powerful forward cut. The impact point on the target occurs when the arms are at their greatest distance forward of the shoulders. The monouchi achieves the height of impact when it is at full extension from the shoulders. Continue to cut while the monouchi exits the intended point of impact. Stop the sword immediately following the kissaki's exit from the target area.

TSUKI—THRUSTING

Sword schools throughout history have incorporated both slashing and thrusting implements as a part of their arsenal. Certain sword schools have placed more emphasis on one approach over the other. The swords that were used for slashing and moving through a crowded battlefield with multiple opponents were generally curved to accommodate the body's propensity to move in circular motions. The swords that were made for dueling with a single opponent tended to be straight to facilitate powerful thrusting actions through the centerline of attack. The shortest distance to the enemy is directly through the centerline of attack. A direct thrust through the centerline forces the enemy to retreat, block or choose an angle off of the centerline in his attempt to recover or counter. This straight line technique gives the swordsman the ability to attack the opponent from the greatest distance. Thrusting may begin from various kamae or it can be the natural end result and follow through of a cutting action. There are times when it is possible to slice with the monouchi or hoshi and thrust with the kissaki simultaneously toward multiple targets on the opponent.

HITOTSU-TE TSUKI—SINGLE-HAND THRUST

1: The correct hand-sword alignment for a one-hand thrust places the right elbow in a direct line with the *kissaki*. The line between the elbow and the kissaki intersects and crosses through the right wrist. The *tsuka* must be placed under the forearm in order for the thrusting power of the hips to be transferred through the elbow directly to the tip of the sword.

3: The energy from when the *koshi* (waist, hips) does a horizontal rotation pushes the right shoulder and elbow forward simultaneously.

2: Thrusting is done with the body. Transfer the power of the rotation of the hips forward while you turn the right hip and shoulder in the direction of the thrust. The right forearm supports and limits the upward motion of the tsuka to stabilize its vertical movement. The right-hand grip stabilizes the horizontal movement. The hip, shoulder, elbow, hand and kissaki all align along the same vertical plane.

MOROTE TSUKI—TWO-HAND THRUST

1: The correct hand-sword alignment for a two-hand thrust places the palms of both hands above the back of the *tsuka*. The hands are placed in the same position as when cutting. The arms extend the distance between the right forearm, and the *tsuka gashira* decreases until the top of the left wrist is parallel to the bottom of the right wrist. The thrusting power of the hips is transferred through both elbows directly to the tip of the sword.

2: Thrusting is done with the body. Transfer the power of the forward push from the hips and shoulders in the direction of the thrust. The line between the center of the body and the *kissaki* intersects and crosses through the tops of both wrists. Both hands stabilize and limit the horizontal movement of the sword. The hips, shoulders, elbows and hands form a triangle with the kissaki as the apex. This configuration forces all of the energy moving forward from the base of the triangle (the hips and shoulders) to be focused at the single point of the kissaki.

3 : The energy of the body's forward motion pushes the hips and shoulders forward simultaneously. Allow the forward energy of the forward motion to move upward through the hips and sword and not downward into the front knee.

CHIBURI—BLOOD REMOVAL

At the completion of each battojutsu waza, a movement is performed that is designed to remove the residue deposited on the blade during the cutting action. This movement is called chiburi. Throughout the Eishin-ryu batto-ho waza, two basic types of chiburi are used. The first chiburi encountered in *junto sono ichi* is the "wet umbrella" method *(kasa no shizuku o harao)*, which gets its name from its resemblance to flinging the water from a wet umbrella. It is a chiburi done in the older set of waza known as the *Omori-ryu seiza no bu*. For this reason, it is often referred to as *Omori-ryu chiburi* or sometimes as *o-chiburi* meaning big chiburi. However, the most common *chiburi* encountered in the Eishin-ryu batto-ho curriculum is the flicking method known as *yoko chiburi* or sometimes *Eishin-ryu chiburi*. It was the favored method of Hasegawa Eishin when he adapted battojutsu to shorter swords during the early Edo period.

Omori-ryu chiburi is distinct in its large circular movement. The downward circular arc of the sword followed by the sudden snap of the right hand closing around the tsuka cause the monouchi and kissaki to snap forward releasing residue from the blade. The final motion must accelerate to a complete stop as the feet come together. Maintain iaigoshi (power in the hips) throughout the chiburi.

OMORI-RYU CHIBURI

1: At the end of a *kirioroshi*, the sword is directly forward of the body. The right and left hand are exerting a push-pull on the *tsuka*. For *shoden waza*, wait for three seconds after the cut has stopped, then begin the *chiburi*. The right hand pushes forward toward the *kissaki* and pushes the *tsuka* forward and out of the left hand.

2: Maintain *zanshin* as the tsuka leaves the left hand. Continue to pull the left hand back to the left hip. Push the kissaki forward at a 45-degree angle while you begin to turn the cutting edge toward the fallen opponent. The *monouchi* maintains cutting pressure at all times. The right arm remains straight throughout this movement.

3: Continue to push upward and around to the right with the right hand. The *ha* continues to turn forward while the right arm reaches shoulder height. Extend the right arm to the right side of the shoulder with the kissaki pointing to the rear at a 45-degree angle.

4: Maintain the position of the right elbow. Bend the elbow and raise the sword upward to the right front corner of the head. The knuckle of the right-hand thumb should be close to the right front corner of the forehead. Relax the right-hand grip as the sword moves upward to the head.

5: Maintain the position of the right elbow while the sword is allowed to swing downward in front of the face toward the left forward corner in a downward circle.

6: The right arm straightens when the sword moves forward along a parallel plane to the body. As the *tsuba* crosses the centerline, begin to tighten the right-hand grip on the sword like when performing *nukitsuke*. Bring the rear foot forward and parallel to the front foot while the right hand finishes tightening its grip. The right hand, sword and foot stop moving at the same time. The right hand is at the same height and forward of the right hip.

7: Finish by stepping back with the right foot. Maintain the relative position of the right arm and sword to the body, and move back as a single unit. Stop with the kissaki in line with the toes of the front foot. Maintain zanshin throughout the entire chiburi.

The most common chiburi found in the battojutsu and kenjutsu waza makes use of a sharp lateral movement toward the right. This powerful snapping action of yoko chiburi is a result of an expansion of the chest and arms followed by a sudden release of the left hand. Correct *shisei* (posture) must be maintained for this expansion to occur. Tension must build through the legs, hips, chest, elbows and hands before releasing the tsuka.

YOKO CHIBURI—SIDE CHIBURI

1: At the completion of *kirioroshi*, the *kissaki* and *monouchi* are parallel to the ground. Loosen the finger of the left hand with the exception of the little finger, which remains tightly hooked around the *tsuka*. Begin to exert an outward pulling motion with both elbows while pressure is created in the hands pulling against the tsuka.

2: When the pressure builds to when the little finger cannot support the tsuka, release the left finger with a snapping pull of the wrist and draw back the left hand to the left hip while the hip retracts in one fluid motion. The sudden release of the left hand causes the right hand to flick the sword to the right on a horizontal plane. The right hand stops the sword quickly, causing any residue to go flying to the side.

Chiburi can be performed from several positions. When the kirioroshi finishes with the kissaki below the level of the tsuba, the kissaki should remain on the same horizontal plane from the beginning to the end of the yoko chiburi. The right hand and tsuba may stay on the same plane, too, or they may travel upward.

In some instances, the kissaki may finish above the level of the tsuba. In this case, the tsuba should remain on the same horizontal plane from the beginning until the end of the flicking motion when the kissaki drops to below the level of the tsuba.

KISSAKI BELOW THE TSUBA

1: Here, the *kissaki* is below the *tsuba* at end of *kirioroshi*.

2: The kissaki maintains the same horizontal plane after *chiburi*.

KISSAKI ABOVE THE TSUBA

1: Here, the *kissaki* is above the *tsuba* at end of *kirioroshi*.

2: The tsuba maintains the same horizontal plane at end of *chiburi*.

NOTO—RESHEATHING

Naturally at some point, it becomes necessary to return the sword to the scabbard. As discussed in an earlier chapter, the highest form of battojutsu is to achieve victory while the sword remains in the scabbard. However, returning it to this benevolent position should not put the swordsman at risk of a surprise attack. Methods of returning the sword to the saya have been developed to allow the swordsman to maintain awareness and the ability to focus on his environment. These noto and the spirit in which they are to be carried out are an indispensable component of battojutsu, kenjutsu and suemonogiri.

At the early stages of training, noto is done slowly. Shoden-level techniques always establish correct angles and postures that will be necessary to later perform *okuden noto*. At the end of kiriroshi in shoden waza, the feet, hips and shoulders face mostly forward with the exception of a minor adjustment for the natural gripping of the sword, which turns the body slightly at an angle. This body position points the mouth of the saya toward the right front corner.

The noto starts by placing the back of the blade near the habaki and on top of the koiguchi that is formed by the left hand thumb and index finger. The sword is then pushed forward quickly to the right diagonal corner and comes to a sudden halt. The kissaki is allowed to drop into the mouth of the saya but does not move backwards into the saya. A brief pause must accompany this action as though the hand and sword were continuing to move forward. After a brief pause, allow the sword to travel back into the saya at the natural speed that the right arm is allowed to relax. As the tsuba gets progressively closer to the saya, the speed of the returning sword should decelerate in *shoden noto*.

The end of okuden kiriroshi finds the body facing a different angle than in shoden kiriroshi. The opening of the knees and hips during the cut cause the saya to rotate to the left directly facing forward toward the fallen opponent. The body stays in this position throughout okuden noto.

The noto starts by pushing the blade forward and then toward the left hand and saya. As the mune area of the sword close to the habaki clears above the top of the koiguchi, the sword is then pushed forward quickly to the front in the direction of the enemy. As the sword travels forward, the back of the monouchi section of the blade is allowed to drop onto the koiguchi formed by the left hand and continues to slide forward until the kissaki slips naturally into the koiguchi. This rapid push of the sword must be accompanied by a perfect alignment with the forward-facing saya. As the kissaki drops into the mouth of the scabbard, the right hand pushes down and back in the direction of the saya, allowing the sword to resheath itself in a single fluid motion. The sword continues back into the saya swiftly until it is two-thirds of the way seated into the saya. While the final third of the sword moves into the saya, the speed of the noto decelerates quickly while the left hand begins to move the saya onto the sword. It is imperative that practitioners master shoden noto before attempting to perform okuden noto. Accidents are not acceptable because of training negligence. The natural progression of speed and timing throughout all stages of training should be an innate evolution of the swordsman's ability. Speed is relative to a practitioner's ability. Practice the noto slowly at first and allow the natural timing to dictate the speed of the technique. Do not force the technique to move at a pace that is uncomfortable or pushes the limits of your control and focus.

Noto while holding the sword with a natural grip *(honte)* is the most common method used in Eishin-ryu batto-ho. The signature characteristic of this particular noto is the position of the cutting edge when the sword is pulled across the hand and returned to the saya. The cutting edge is turned upward and stands on the back of the sword as it rests on the left hand. This position is referred to as *tate-ha* (standing edge) because the edge of the sword appears to stand upright.

PROCEDURE FOR HONTE (STANDARD-GRIP NOTO)

1: At the end of *chiburi,* turn the bottom of the *saya* toward your body. Align the *koiguchi* (mouth of the *saya*) with the forearm. This will turn the line formed by the index finger and thumb into alignment with the radial bone on the top of the arm.

2: Place the back of the sword on the web of the left hand and in alignment with the left elbow. Do not allow the sword to cross the line formed by the forearm and the hand. Injury to the left hand usually occurs when the sword is misaligned during this stage of noto.

INCORRECT SWORD AND HAND ALIGNMENT

CONTINUED ON NEXT PAGE

3: Push the sword forward until the backside of the *kissaki* slides across the web of the left hand.

4: Allow the kissaki to travel forward until the tip is able to drop down between the thumb and index finger of the left hand. Open the hole that is formed by the fingers and allow the kissaki to rest in the saya.

5: Pull back the web of the left hand to prevent it from being cut while you insert the remaining length of the sword into the saya.

STANDARD NOTO

1: The standard grip *noto* starts at the sword's position following *chiburi*.

2: Push the opening on the *saya* forward to the middle of the body with the left hand. Form a *koiguchi* (fish mouth) over the opening at the end of the saya. Be sure to align the opening line on the koiguchi with the radial bone of the left wrist.

3: Push the sword forward around the body and place the back of the sword (*mune*) on the top of the *koiguchi* that is formed by the left thumb and left index finger. Release the tight grip with the right hand when the weight of the sword is transferred to the top of the left hand. The mune makes contact with the left hand a few inches back from the *habaki*. Place the sword on the top of the hand and forearm. The sword will stand on the left hand vertically with the *ha* turned upward. In this position, the back of the mune should be correctly lined up with the forearm and elbow.

4: Use the right hand to quickly push the *tsuka* forward on the same diagonal plane as the saya. Stop when the *tsuka gashira* is in line with the right hip. The sword should remain parallel to the ground. At the same time, pull back the left hip and push the saya back along the line of the hip to allow the *kissaki* to align with the koiguchi. Pause for a moment in this position.

CONTINUED ON NEXT PAGE

5: Open the "mouth" that is formed by your left thumb and index finger. Allow the kissaki to drop into the opening. The *kissaki mune* (backside of the *kissaki*) rests on the inside of the *saya* and inside your index finger.

6: Push downward with the right arm to push the kissaki into the saya. Keep the right arm straight with the wrist bent slightly downward while the sword moves back toward the center and into the saya.

7: When two-thirds of the blade has been resheathed in the scabbard, begin to push the saya forward with the left hand. The left hand and saya meet the *tsuba* at the centerline of the body.

8: Reach up with the left thumb and pull back on the tsuba to reseat the *habaki* into the *kuchigane* (throat of the saya).

9: Push the right hand forward on the top of the *tsuka* until it reaches the *tsuka gashira*.

Gyakute noto also uses the tate-ha (standing-edge noto). This style of noto is usually performed after a drip-style chiburi, meaning it follows the practice of *happo-giri* (eight-directional cut). It is not found in the Eishin-ryu batto-ho waza but is included anyway as a necessary basic technique for those who wish to pursue further study.

PROCEDURE FOR GYAKUTE (REVERSE-GRIP NOTO)

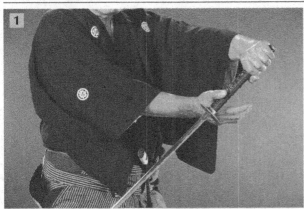

1: At the end of a downward cut, the execution of a drip *chiburi* ends with the *mune* resting on the knee and the hand drawn upward in front of the body.

2: Reverse the position of the right hand to the opposite side *(omote)* of the *tsuka*. Grasp the tsuka with the right hand so that the heel of the palm is in contact with the outer ring of the *tsuba*.

CONTINUED ON NEXT PAGE

3: Support the weight of the sword with the right hand. Release the left hand from the *tsuka* and form a *koiguchi* (fish mouth) on the end of the *saya*.

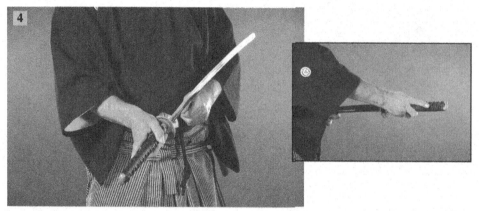

4: Swing the sword forward and around and behind the left hip. Allow the right hand to slip around the tsuka to the *ura* side (inside right) of the sword when the cutting edge is turned upward during the swing. Maintain contact with the palm of the hand on the tsuba while you make this transition with your hand. Place the right index finger along the inside of the tsuka, pointing toward the *tsuka gashira*. Place the back edge of the sword on top of the left hand and forearm. The sword should touch the left hand just behind the *habaki*.

5: Turn the left hip forward while the sword is pushed diagonally forward in the direction of your right index finger and tsuka gashira. Allow the back of the sword to slide over the *koiguchi* and forearm as it travels forward. Stop the forward motion of the sword when the *kissaki* crosses over the web of the left hand and the tsuka gashira is directly forward of the right hip.

6: Open the "mouth" that is formed by your left thumb and index finger. Allow the kissaki to drop into the opening. The *kissaki mune* (back side of the kissaki) rests on the inside of the saya and inside your index finger.

7: Push downward with the right arm to push the kissaki into the saya. Keep the right arm straight with the wrist bent slightly inward while the sword moves back toward the center and into the saya.

8: When two-thirds of the blade has been replaced in the scabbard, begin to push the saya forward with the left hand. The left hand meets the tsuba at the centerline of the body.

GYAKUTE NOTO—REVERSE GRIP

1: At the completion of drip *chiburi*, the right foot is forward, and the sword is inclined at an upward diagonal angle to the left with the cutting edge facing forward. The *mune* rests on the right thigh.

2: Reverse the right-hand grip from the bottom to the top of the sword's handle. Keep both arms extended and straight.

3: Place the left hand on the mouth of the *saya*. Control the sword with the right hand as the left hand lowers to the saya to form the *koiguchi*.

4: Push the mouth of the saya forward in line with the center of the body and in line with the *tsuba* and right hand. Lift the sword from the right knee with the right hand.

CONTINUED ON NEXT PAGE

5: Swing the *kissaki* forward and around the front of the body at waist height in a cutting fashion with the cutting edge of the sword facing forward. Reverse the position of the right hand to the *ura* side of the handle with the index finger extended. (See preliminary practice on page 108.)

6: Place the sword on the left hand. Place the back of the blade on the koiguchi and forearm at the center of the body.

7: Rotate the right hip clockwise toward the front as you push the *tsuka gashira* forward at a 45-degree angle. Do not pass the outside of the right hip with the end of the sword handle. Allow the kissaki to slide over the web of the left hand between the thumb and index finger. Keep the sword parallel to the ground.

8: As the kissaki slides past the web of your left hand, open the "mouth" that is formed by your left thumb and index finger. Allow the kissaki to drop into the opening. The *kissaki mune* (back side of the kissaki) rests on the inside of the saya and on the palm side of your index finger.

9: Push downward with the right arm to push the kissaki into the saya. Keep the right arm straight with the wrist bent slightly downward while the sword moves back toward the center and into the saya.

10: Push the saya forward to meet the right hand. When two-thirds of the blade has been replaced in the scabbard, begin to push the saya forward with the left hand. The left hand meets the tsuba at the centerline of the body.

11: Reach up with the left thumb and pull back on the tsuba to reseat the *habaki* (collar) into the *kuchigane* (throat of the saya). Pull back the tsuba with the thumb.

12: Push the right hand forward along the side of the *tsuka* until it reaches the tsuka gashira. Allow the thumb to cover the tsuka gashira when it comes to the end of the handle.

TAI-SABAKI—BODY MOVEMENT

Combat is dynamic and everchanging. The ability to adapt to the improvisational movements of the enemy can be frustrating if the body has not been trained to move in all directions. Balance, control, footwork and timing become the novice and advanced practitioner's focus of study. Although there are innumerable combinations of footwork available to the budoka, they are all just variations of normal stepping and moving patterns you are accustomed to doing. The difference is in having to do them in conjunction with the enemy's footwork and timing. The ability to move gracefully and in conjunction with proper shisei (posture), kuzushi (balance) and yoyu (ability to change) must be mastered.

A budoka's commitment to the study of tai-sabaki (body movement) is no less daunting than that of a professional dancer. The similarity to dance is quite predictable. It may be easy to step onto a dance floor by yourself and move around somewhat naturally. But anyone who has attempted to learn how to dance with a partner in a predetermined pattern may have found that stepping naturally is a challenge. Now imagine not knowing what dance your partner was going to do. Imagine that each step he took could lead into a new dance that you've never seen before. Complicate things further by giving your dance partner a sword with the mission to cut you down as you dance together. How many people would want to dance with a partner like this without scores of lessons in footwork and movement?

The phrase *"ashi no ura ni hanshi ichi mai"* describes a very important principle of movement that is well-known to practitioners of kenjutsu and *kendo* in Japan. Because battojutsu is essentially an aspect of kenjutsu, it is very important for all practitioners of battojutsu to understand and incorporate this principle into their practice. *Ashi no ura* refers to the bottom of the foot. *Hanshi* is fine rice paper used for *sumi-e* and *shodo*. *Ichi mai* means "one." So, "ashi no ura ni hanshi ichi mai" means that there is space for one sheet of paper between the bottom of the feet and the floor. This is a reference to the proper method of *ashi-sabaki* (footwork) in battojutsu and kenjutsu. The feeling of "ashi no ura ni hanshi ichi mai" is that of having the feet on the floor but not on the floor—a feeling of gliding when moving. This concept means that your weight is not loaded or fixed in any single spot. Instead, you're able to move freely and effortlessly in any direction. This is critical whether attacking or defending against an attack. A swordsman must be able to move instantly to attack while ideally expressing the concept of *issoku itto*—one step, one cut.

To properly utilize "ashi no ura ni hanshi ichi mai," the body must not only be light and fluid but also firm in order to properly make the cut or strike. This is very hard to do, especially in kenjutsu and its requirements for proper shisei. Shisei, or correct posture and attitude, are fundamental to sword practice. It pervades in everything that is done and is just as important as the principle of "ashi no ura ni hanshi ichi mai."

As you strive to acquire the feeling for proper ashi-sabaki, you must simultaneously avoid *itsuku* (being stuck or being frozen in place). This is one of the things that can severely impact your budo, and obviously in face-to-face combat, it would have had dire consequences. To avoid itsuku, avoid deep stances. It is difficult, if not impossible, to move effortlessly from deep postures. The exception to this is when you move into the so-called "power stance" while executing a final kirioroshi. The importance of good ashi-sabaki, especially that which reflects "ashi no ura ni hanshi ichi mai" cannot be stressed enough. No matter if you practice battojutsu, kenjutsu or other budo, proper ashi-sabaki is a key foundation. It's easy to judge the quality of a budoka by his ashi-sabaki because it's hard to hide poor stances or poor footwork. Conversely, effortlessness of motion is the result of proper kamae, shisei, ashi-sabaki, and an understanding of "ashi no ura ni hanshi ichi mai."

AYUMI-ASHI—STEPPING PATTERN

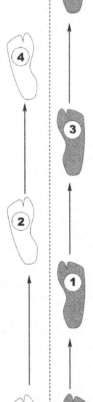

◄ *Ayumi-ashi* **is the natural walking pattern of most people. It is the continual cross-step pattern we use in our everyday activities.**

1: *Ayumi-ashi* begins naturally and is the primary way that people propel themselves forward and back. Start in a natural and relaxed posture with feet together.

2: When wearing a sword, the *Eishin-ryu* swordsman always takes the first step forward with the right foot. Step forward with your right foot and place the foot down naturally. Allow the weight of the body to balance equally over both feet.

3: Walk naturally forward with the left foot. The left foot passes by the right foot and assumes the forward position.

4: Walk naturally forward with the right foot. The right foot passes by the left foot and assumes the forward position.

TSUKI-ASHI—THRUSTING STEP

◄ *Tsuki-ashi* is the method that is used to shuffle forward and backward.

1: Start in a natural relaxed posture with your feet together.

2: Take the first step forward with the right foot. Allow the weight of the body to balance equally over both feet.

3: Push the right foot forward with power from the left foot.

4: After the forward thrust with the right foot, allow the left foot to slide forward.

CONTINUED ON NEXT PAGE

5: Push the right foot forward with power from the left foot.

TENSHIN—TURN AND EVADE

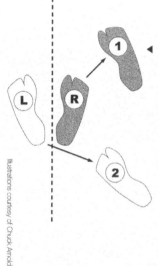

◀ *Tenshin* is the movement that is used to evade an oncoming attack or to counter a strong *kamae* that is in control of the centerline.

1: Start in *jodan no kamae* with feet together.

2: Take the first step to the right side using *tsuki-ashi* with the right foot off of the centerline. Shift the weight of the body over the right foot for balance.

3: Shift to the right and cut. Rotate the hips and shoulders counterclockwise and allow the rear left foot to shift to right rear corner behind the left hip off of the centerline of attack.

IRIMI-TENSHIN—TURN AND EVADE

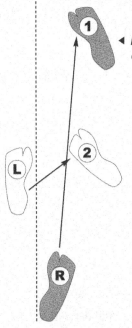

◄ *Irimi-tenshin* is the movement that is used to move through the centerline, then evade an oncoming attack while you counterattack from off of the centerline.

1: Begin in *jodan no kamae* with the left foot forward. Pressure the centerline of attack with your spirit and cutting energy in the *monouchi*.

2: Step forward in *ayumi-ashi* with the right foot while you threaten to cut *kirioroshi*.

3: Step directly forward on the centerline of attack with the right foot. In mid-stride, slide the right foot diagonally forward off of the centerline. Allow the weight of the body to shift to the right to follow the right foot forward.

4: Rotate the hips and shoulders counterclockwise and allow the rear left foot to shift to the right behind the left hip.

CHAPTER 6

OFFENSIVE AND DEFENSIVE
APPLICATION OF FUNDAMENTALS

Each sword technique, depending on whether it is performed with a single hand or two, changes the relative vulnerability of every target. Although specific targets may be lethal when cut with the monouchi, they may be totally unaffected when cutting with the kissaki. Likewise, other targets may lie in a protected area or be too small for the monouchi to reach. In addition, there is a difference between the power that is generated during a one-hand cut and its two-hand counterpart. A similar disparity also occurs for each method when choosing the cutting distance. The kiri-ma (cutting distance) to the target changes depending on whether you can use a single or double-hand technique. The power that each technique is capable of generating also influences which targets are available to the swordsman.

SUKI—OPENINGS AND TARGETS

Sword smiths fashioned kissaki that were short *(ko-kissaki)*, mid-length *(chu-kissaki)* or quite long *(o-kissaki)*. Which length was used depended on the personal preference of the practitioner and his affinity for a particular mode of fighting. Regardless of the length, the kissaki is only able to cut as deep as the hoshi of the sword will permit, which means most cuts with the kissaki are not enough to finish the encounter; they need to be followed by another blow. Thus, certain targets are more common to cut at with particular techniques.

TARGET AREAS FOR THE KISSAKI (ONE-HAND CUTS)

1: Apply *suihei* horizontally across the eyes.

2: Cut *kiriage* diagonally upward across the body.

3: The *kesa-giri* is delivered diagonally and downward across the face.

4: A *suihei* can also be cut horizontally to the body.

The monouchi, which is the third of the blade behind the kissaki, affords the deepest and most powerful cut when a two-hand grip is engaged. It is capable of cutting through massive targets when the body and arms are generating sufficient energy. However, the limited amount of energy generated by the use of a single-hand grip substantially diminishes the potential cutting power of the blade. In this case, it is critical to know the specified targets that the monouchi is capable of slicing.

TARGET AREAS FOR THE MONOUCHI (ONE-HAND CUTS)

1: Cut *kesa-giri* diagonally downward to the neck.

2: Apply kesa-giri diagonally and downward to the raised forearms.

3: Apply a *suihei* horizontally to the biceps and triceps of the upper arm.

4: *Kiriage* is applied diagonally and upward to the forearm, wrist or hand.

All of the targets that are available to single-hand attacks with the kissaki and monouchi can also be targeted using a two-hand grip. In addition to the targets available to single-hand cuts, there are the areas of the body that can be effectively cut by using the full power of both arms with an improved connection to the hips.

TARGET AREAS FOR THE MONOUCHI (TWO-HAND CUTS)

1: *Kirioroshi* can be applied directly forward and down to the top of the head.

2: A *kesa-giri* cuts diagonally downward to the top of the shoulder.

3: Cut *suihei* horizontally across the torso.

4: Apply *kiriage* diagonally upward to the forearm, wrist or hand.

Both hands can also be used as supplemental support on areas of the sword other than the tsuka. Following a cut to the side of the neck or body with a single-hand cut, you may use the left hand to support and add power to the *monouchi*. This technique opens the door to a powerful horizontal, upward or downward finishing cut.

MONOUCHI—SUPPORTING HAND (SOETE)

1: Reach forward with the left hand and place it on the back of the sword behind the *monouchi*. Apply forward pressure against the monouchi with the left hand while pulling the monouchi and *kissaki* across the target.

BOGYO WAZA—DEFENSIVE TECHNIQUES

Present within the kenjutsu fundamentals of Eishin-ryu are varied strategies for responding to attacks dependent on the swordman's position and the route that the enemy takes to affect his strike. Defensive moves can be delineated and categorized according to their timing, direction and intent. The most opportune moment to cut the enemy does not always occur before the opponent seizes the initiative and delivers his attacks. The need to defend an oncoming siege leaves little room for error in judgment or timing before counterattacking.

A defensive maneuver that places the practitioner in the position of having to receive a cut directly on the edge of the blade in a blocking fashion is considered the least desirable. This method is also looked on as being the most defensive in nature. It may be understood that attacks that are parried or deflected allow the defender the opportunity to absorb and respond to his enemy's charge simultaneously. And lastly, if the defender has the opportunity to lure or attack his enemy while he is defending an oncoming affront, the defense actually becomes offensive in nature.

Sen is the term used to denote "initiative" in which it evolves through a process of converting intention into movement. The combatant that establishes the initiative to strike first is prone to controlling the combative space even before he moves. This offensive intent leads in most cases to techniques that are offensive in nature. The defender who has lost the sen to his opponent must respond to the attack in a defensive role before he is able to regain combative neutrality. To move and respond after the initiative of the attack has been seized is referred to as *"go no sen."*

A more desirable environment is one in which the defender's intent is firm and his intuition is adequate to seize on the enemy's intention. Then the defender can move to forestall the enemy's attack when it is launched. This is known as *"sen no sen."* A scenario such as this finds the defender moving in conjunction with his opponent's attack. Both combatants seize the initiative and they each initiate movements in tandem with each other.

The third condition finds the intended defender initiating the counterattack even before the enemy has formulated the offensive technique in his mind. This occurs even though the adversary's intention to attack is strong and present. In fact, the enemy's strong intention and his urge to take the initiative is the necessary ingredient that the defender senses. It makes it possible for the keen defender to steal the initiative from him and to attack him at his weakest moment. This asphyxiation of the enemy's intention and using it to launch the pracititoner's own attack is known as *"sen sen no sen."* The defender seizes his attacker's intention to launch an attack. He then smothers the enemy's ability to initiate by launching an offensive technique of his own. The individual that is playing the role of the losing combatant in training is referred to as the *uchitachi*. The role that is taken by the winner is referred to as *shitachi*. The more defensive methods of blocking and receiving an attack come to us from the Shimomura-ha tradition and the more aggressive *bogyo waza* techniques represent the spirit of the Tanimura-ha. The Tanimura-ha approach to blocking employs an offensive spirit when attacking. Move forward to greet the attack and control the combative space from under uchitachi's sword. This is "sen no sen" response.

Blocking in the Shimomura-ha tradition entails receiving the attacker's sword in a defensive maneuver. When performing the technique from this tradition, it is recommended to move away from the attack and cover the centerline. This action occurs as the defender's sword moves upward to receive his opponent's attacking blade. This is a "go no sen" form of response.

AGE UKE—RISING BLOCK (TANIMURA-HA SEN NO SEN)

1: **Uchitachi:** Assume *jodan no kamae* with the left foot forward.

Shitachi: Assume *gedan no kamae* with the right foot forward.

2: **Uchitachi:** Shuffle forward with the left foot and begin to step the right foot forward to cut.

Shitachi: Pull the left foot forward directly toward the right foot while the hips draw upward. Raise the sword. Move both hands upward toward the left side corner of the left shoulder and above the head height. The sword moves upward and across the body.

3: **Uchitachi:** Cut quickly when the forward movement of *shitachi* invades the cutting space.

Shitachi: Against *uchitachi*, catch the power of his sword with the power of your rising hips. Receive uchitachi's sword with the cutting edge of the blade just to the left of the center curvature of the sword. In the final position, the *kissaki* is to the right front and the *tsuka* is to the left front. The sword crosses the front of your body and is horizontal to the floor.

AGE UKE—RISING BLOCK (SHIMOMURA-HA GO NO SEN)

1: **Uchitachi:** Assume *jodan no kamae* with the left foot forward.

Shitachi: Assume *gedan no kamae* with the right foot forward.

2: **Uchitachi:** Shuffle forward with the left foot and begin to step the right foot forward to cut.

Shitachi: Shuffle back with the left, then pull the right foot back directly toward the left foot while the hips draw upward and raise the sword. Move both hands upward toward the left side corner of the left shoulder and above the head height. The sword moves upward and across the body.

3: **Uchitachi:** Follow the retreating movement of *shitachi* and cut to the head.

Shitachi: Against *uchitachi*, catch the power of his sword with the power of your rising hips. Receive uchitachi's sword with the cutting edge of the blade just to the left of the center curvature. In the final position, the *kissaki* is to the right front and the *tsuka* is to the left front. The sword crosses the front of the body and is horizontal to the floor.

5

YOKO UKE/TSUBAZERIAI— SIDE BLOCK/HAND GUARDS MEET (SHIMOMURA-HA GO NO SEN)

1: Uchitachi: Assume *chudan no kamae* with the right foot forward.

Shitachi: Assume chudan no kamae with the right foot forward.

2: Uchitachi: Shuffle forward with the right foot in *tsuki-ashi* and begin to thrust forward to *shitachi* at his throat.

Shitachi: Shuffle back with the left foot, then pull the right foot back directly toward the left foot while the hips draw upward and you raise your sword. Against *uchitachi*, begin to allow his sword to ride up on the cutting edge of your sword and pull your hands back toward the left side. The sword moves upward and across your body while tilted at an angle forward to the right corner.

3: Uchitachi: Follow shitachi's retreating movement while thrusting forward.

Shitachi: Catch the power of uchitachi's sword with the power of the rising hips. Guide uchitachi's sword upward and just to the left of your head with the cutting edge of your blade. In the final position, the blocking sword's *kissaki* is to the right upper front corner and the right hand is level with your left shoulder. The sword crosses the front of the body and is held at a position diagonally to the floor.

4: Uchitachi: When the sword is fully extended, move your elbows downward while shitachi attempts to move in and control the combative space.

Shitachi: Move in to control the combative space. As uchitachi overextends his thrust to the side, shuffle forward with your right foot and push the *monouchi* downward to cut toward uchitachi's left shoulder and neck.

CONTINUED ON NEXT PAGE

5: **Uchitachi:** Push forward with the hips while the swords are pushed to the sides. Lower the arms to the center of the body at chest level. Receive shitachi's downward attack with the sword held in front. Make contact at *tsuba* to tsuba.

Shitachi: Move the hips fully forward to meet uchitachi's downward-moving sword. Allow the sword to ride down the side of uchitachi's blade until the tsuba collides with uchitachi's tsuba. As the sword moves in and down, maintain control on top of uchitachi's tsuba. Maintain cutting pressure toward the opponent's neck and shoulder. Maintain the top position above uchitachi's tsuba while the swords move forward and collide.

6: **Uchitachi:** Push forward to cut and try to find the weak spot in shitachi's center.

Shitachi: Push forward to cut and try to find the weak spot in uchitachi's center.

Another form of receiving and defending from a thrust entails sweeping the blade aside. As the opponent thrusts through the center, his sword is swept aside with the side of the *shinogi*. The practitioner cuts to the opponent's head. The final cut to the head must be timed to coincide with the end of the attacker's thrust.

HARAI UKE—SWEEPING BLOCK (SEN NO SEN)

1: **Uchitachi:** Assume *chudan no kamae* with the right foot forward. Cross swords with *shitachi* on the *omote* (left side) of the blade near the *monouchi*.

Shitachi: Assume *chudan no kamae* with the right foot forward. Cross swords with *uchitachi* on the omote (left side) of the blade near the monouchi.

2: Uchitachi: Pressure shitachi's sword to feel for an opening. Push the hips forward in *tsuki-ashi* and begin to thrust to shitachi's solar plexus.

Shitachi: As you feel uchitachi pressure forward on your sword, turn the wrists counterclockwise to allow uchitachi's sword to begin to slide on the *shinogi* of the sword.

3: Uchitachi: Continue to shuffle forward, leading with the right foot. Thrust forward through the centerline with the *kissaki*.

Shitachi: As uchitachi attempts to thrust through the centerline, step forward to the right in a *tenshin* movement. Push downward with the *mune* against the back of uchitachi's sword and sweep *(harai)* it downward to the left, past your left side.

4: Uchitachi: As shitachi pushes downward, continue to push forward through the line of the attack.

Shitachi: As uchitachi's sword pushes past the left hip, continue to move forward to the front right corner and remove your left hip from the line of the oncoming attack. Sweep the mune of the sword to the left and upward in an arc along the left side of the body. Follow through with the sword in a continual arc through *jodan.* The cutting edge of the blade should face uchitachi throughout the entire sweeping motion.

CONTINUED ON NEXT PAGE

5: Uchitachi: Follow through with the kissaki toward the original point of the intended target.

Shitachi: Continue to cut in a large diagonal circle to the right from the corner. Cut to uchitachi's head when the thrust stops moving forward.

6: Uchitachi: Follow through to the throat height of your intended target.

Shitachi: Continue to move forward and cut down *kesa-giri* to uchitachi's left shoulder region. Make contact with the shoulder with the monouchi near the intersection of uchitachi's neck and shoulder.

UKENAGASHI—FLOWING BLOCK (GO NO SEN)

1: Uchitachi: Assume *jodan no kamae* with the left foot forward.

Shitachi: With the sword still in the *saya*, step forward with the left foot diagonally to the right front corner and draw the sword one third of the way out.

2: Uchitachi: Shuffle forward and cut downward in *kirioroshi* toward *shitachi's* left shoulder.

Shitachi: Step right foot directly to the right rear corner as you continue to draw the sword upward. Move the right hand upward toward the right front corner of the right shoulder at head height. The sword moves upward on the same plane it was at it rested in the saya. In the final position the *kissaki* is at the height of the bottom of the left ear. The sword crosses the front of the body at a downward angle.

3: Uchitachi: Continue to shuffle forward with your leading left foot. Cut forward through the centerline with the *monouchi*.

Shitachi: As *uchitachi* attempts to cut through the center-line, rotate the hips and shoulders counterclockwise and lean the upper body back toward the right rear corner. Turn the right hand clockwise to deflect uchitachi's sword with the *shinogi* of the blade while pulling back the left hip and shoulder. Push the shinogi against the outer side of uchitachi's sword and allow it to flow to the left and past the left side of the body. Continue to rotate counterclockwise and allow the rotation to swing the *kissaki* into a cutting position behind the head.

4: Uchitachi: As *shitachi's* sword slips away to the left, continue to cut forward through the line of the attack.

Shitachi: As uchitachi's sword cuts past the left hip, step the right foot forward and parallel to the left foot. Cut *kiritsuke* to uchitachi's head. Begin the cut with the right hand and add stability to the cut by assisting with the left hand.

As the opponent attempts to attack with *kiriroshi*, move forward aggressively while raising the sword to cut. As the swords make contact, push through the opponents centerline and cut him down. This is *"sen sen no sen."*

SURIAGE UKE—PUSHING UPWARD BLOCK (SEN SEN NO SEN)

1: Uchitachi: Assume *jodan no kamae* with the right foot forward.

Shitachi: Assume *gedan no kamae* with the right foot forward and begin to raise the sword upward through *chudan no kamae.*

2: Uchitachi: Step forward on the left foot and cut *kiriroshi* to the head of *shitachi*.

Shitachi: As *uchitachi* begins his cut, shuffle forward with the lead right foot to cut through the centerline. Raise the *monouchi* directly up through the centerline of uchitachi's oncoming attack. Make contact with uchitachi's sword on the *omote* side of the blade. When contact is made with uchitachi's sword, quickly turn the wrists clockwise and allow the curvature of the blade to deflect the oncoming attack to the left. The upward motion of the arms should continue to "push" forward and through this process. Do not pull back from the elbows. As the body moves directly forward, the arms should move directly up the centerline.

3: Uchitachi: Continue to shuffle forward with your leading left foot cutting forward through the centerline with the monouchi.

Shitachi: Move forward with the body and push upward with the sword to create a wedging effect through the centerline with the upward swinging sword. Push upward until the kissaki is 90 degrees upward and the arms are fully extended. The sword stops its upward movement forward of the head.

4: Uchitachi: As shitachi pushes upward, continue to cut forward through the line of the attack while your sword is deflected to the right.

Shitachi: As uchitachi's sword cuts past the left hip, continue to move forward through the centerline and cut to the front of uchitachi's head.

HAPPO-GIRI—EIGHT-DIRECTION CUT

The sword retains the ability to cut in an infinite number of planes around the body. Your cutting space (kiri-ma) is the distance away from the body that the trajectory of the arc of the kissaki travels along.

Imagine standing within an invisible sphere of protection. It is a three-dimensional geometric form that is made up of an infinite number of two-dimensional circular planes around the body. This sphere extends outward to the distance reachable by means of the kissaki. When you divide the sphere into eight equal quadrants, each dividing line represents a cutting plane around the body. Although there are an infinite number of these circular planes, this chapter presents eight of them that represent the kiri-ma between a swordsman and his opponent.

The following drill of happo-giri (eight-direction cut) establishes a fundamental repertoire of cutting angles in addition to a comprehension of the cutting sphere. The illustration on page 130 depicts the cutting sphere divided into eight sections. The lines that divide these sections are the cutting planes for the happo-giri drill. The numbers at the end of the outer lines represent the order in which they are performed. The arrowheads represent the directions of the cuts.

EIGHT ANGLES OF ATTACK

1. left-to-right nukitsuke
2. downward kirioroshi
3. left-to-right kiriage
4. right-to-left kesa-giri
5. left-to-right yoko-ichimonji
6. right-to-left kiriage
7. left-to-right kesa-giri
8. right-to-left yoko-ichimonji

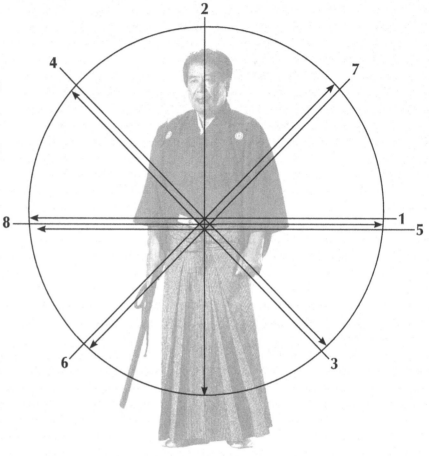

HAPPO-GIRI (EIGHT-DIRECTION CUTTING DRILL)

1: Start standing naturally with your hands at the side of the body.

2: Grasp the sword with the left hand at the *saya*.

3: Push downward on the saya as the right hand grabs the *tsuka*.

4: Turn the body to the left and push the sword upward with the left hand. The left hand pulls back the saya.

5: When two-thirds of the blade has been drawn, step forward with the right foot and continue to open the hip as the *tsuka gashira* moves slightly to the left.

6: Cut horizontally across the chest. This cut is referred to as *suihei* (flat water) or *yoko-ichimonji* (single line to sideways).

7: Perform *furikaburi.* Push the *kissaki* forward then back toward the left ear. Maintain power in the kissaki.

8: Raise the sword and prepare to cut from above the head.

9: Perform a *kirioroshi* directly down the centerline.

10: Move the kissaki to the lower rear left corner. The cutting edge should face down and forward. Move left into *hidari waki no kamae.*

11: Cut *kiriage* diagonally upward from left to right.

12: Stop the diagonal upward cut at 45 degrees forward and above you right shoulder.

CONTINUED ON NEXT PAGE

13: Turn the hands and reverse the cutting edge downward at a 45-degree angle.

14: Cut *kesa-giri* downward right to left on the same 45-degree angle.

15: Stop the downward kesa-giri at 45 degrees outside of the left knee.

16: Move the sword to the left horizontal side. Raise the sword to the rear left parallel to the ground at waist height.

17: Extend the sword away from the body to the left as you begin the cut. Turn the hips clockwise and cut yoko-ichimonji from left to right. Maintain a level plane with the *hasuji*.

18: Cut through the centerline. As the sword crosses the centerline, maintain equal weight distribution on both feet. Pivot from the center of the hips.

19: Stop the horizontal cut at 90 degrees to the right side of the body. Do not allow the weight to shift from the left leg to the right leg while the cut is performed.

20: Move the kissaki to the lower rear right corner. The cutting edge should face down and forward and move right in to *migi waki no kamae*.

21: Cut kiriage diagonally upward from right to left.

22: Stop the diagonal upward cut at 45 degrees forward and above you left shoulder. Turn the hands and reverse the cutting edge downward at a 45-degree angle.

23: Reverse the sword angle.

24: Cut with *kesa-giri* downward and left to right on the same 45-degree angle.

25: Stop at 45 degrees at the downward right. Stop the downward kesa-giri outside of the right knee. Raise the sword to the rear right and parallel to the ground at waist height.

26: Step forward with the right foot. Spread the feet wide apart but equidistant to the center of the body. Extend the sword away from the body to the right as you begin the cut. Turn the hips clockwise and cut yoko-ichimonji from right to left.

27: Cut through the centerline. As the sword crosses the centerline, maintain equal weight distribution on both feet. Pivot from the center of the hips. Maintain a level plane with the hasuji.

28: Stop the horizontal cut at 90 degrees to the left side of the body. Do not allow the weight to shift from the right leg to the left leg while the cut is performed.

29: Take two steps back to *chudan no kamae*. Step back with the right foot and then step back with the left foot while the sword travels though *jodan* to chudan no kamae.

30: Reverse the position of the right hand to the top of the tsuka in preparation for a reverse-hand *noto*.

CONTINUED ON NEXT PAGE

31: Place the sword on the left hand at the *koiguchi* and perform *gyakute* (reversed hand) *noto*.

32: Maintain *zanshin* while the *tsuba* meets the saya during noto.

33: Move the right hand forward to the tsuka gashira. Then step forward with the left foot parallel to the right foot.

34: Release the right hand from the tsuka.

35: Release the left hand from the saya.

CHAPTER 7
EISHIN-RYU BATTO-HO WAZA

The formalized waza of Eishin-ryu batto-ho were developed as standing forms to instruct new swordsman in the correct methods of Japanese sword drawing. The 12 waza demonstrated in this chapter are practiced today throughout the world and form the fundamental core instruction for those wishing to gain and assimilate proper movement and cutting technique. These *waza* were introduced in July 1939 by the 20th Eishin-ryu *soke* (headmaster), Kono Hyakuren, of the main line of *Muso jikiden eishin-ryu* in compliance with the request of the Dai Nihon Butoku Kai. The directive was to institute a training regimen for acolytes studying at the Budo Senmon Gakko, which had been established at the Butokuden. These waza were based on and drawn from the older koryu waza of Muso jikiden eishin-ryu.

The Eishin-ryu batto-ho waza sets are comprised of seven basic (shoden) forms and five high-level (okuden) forms. The first seven waza are classified as shoden-level instruction and should conform to the information presented in chapters five and six. The waza known as *shihoto sono ni* was added to the curriculum by the 21st soke of Eishin-ryu, Fukui Seizan. The shoden method establishes the correct positioning of the body during the nukitsuke, kirioroshi, chiburi and noto. This level of instruction establishes a baseline for the mechanical skills needed when later executing the okuden method. These shoden waza prepare the swordsman to correctly move and manipulate the timing and distance relative to his opponent.

The first okuden waza presented in this book, *zentekigyakuto sono ichi*, was added to this set by *hanshi* Shimabukuro Masayuki who is the 21st *soshihan* of the Muso jikiden eishin-ryu to compliment and conform to the stepping patterns established in *junto sono ichi* of the shoden set. Thus, it establishes a Tanimura-ha approach to the waza. The waza in this set capture and define the deeper levels of movement and strategy. They reveal the true understanding of both the Shimomura and Tanimura methods of Eishin-ryu swordsmanship.

HAPPO-GIRI (EIGHT-DIRECTION CUTTING DRILL)

Shoden Kata	Junto Sono Ichi Junto Sono Ni Tsuigekito Shato Shihoto Sono Ichi Shihoto Sono Ni Zantotsuto
Okuden Kata	Zentekigyakuto Sono Ichi Zentekigyakuto Sono Ni Tatekito Kotekigyakuto Kotekinukiuchi

JUNTO SONO ICHI—ORDERED SWORD FORM NO. 1

While you are walking, an opponent to your forward position attempts to cut you. To stop his attack, you perform nukitsuke to cut his chest, arm or throat. Then you move forward, pursuing him. You cut down toward the head of your retreating opponent while stepping forward with your left leg. Perform chiburi and replace the sword in the scabbard. Return to your original position.

JUNTO SONO ICHI—HOW TO DRAW THE SWORD

1: Step forward with the right foot and grab the *saya* with the left hand.

2: Step forward with the left foot and grab the *tsuka* with the right hand.

3: Step forward with the right foot while performing *nukiuchi* to your opponent's chest.

4: Swing your sword up over your head with your right hand. Your left hand joins your right hand on the tsuka in *furikaburi*.

5: Step your left leg forward and cut down to your opponent from overhead. The sword should stop parallel to the ground at your waist height.

6: Perform *o-chiburi*, stepping your right leg forward to join your left leg in *musubiashi*. The sword tip should stop moving when your feet come together.

7: Face the right toes to the front and shift your left leg backward.

CONTINUED ON NEXT PAGE

8: Push the saya forward to the middle of your body and perform *shoden noto.*

9: Grip the *tsuka gashira* and step your left leg forward to join your right leg in musubiashi. Raise your eyes to look at the *shomen.* Until this time, you sould have been looking at your fallen opponent.

10: Release your right hand from the tsuka gashira and bring it to the side of your right thigh. Step back, starting with your left leg, in five steps to your original starting position.

11: Stop and release your left hand from the *koiguchi.* Retur to a natural standing posture.

JUNTO SONO NI—ORDERED SWORD FORM NO. 2

While you are walking, an opponent to your forward position attempts to cut you. To stop his attack, you directly cut his chest, arm or head. Then you cut down toward the head of the retreating opponent while stepping forward with your right leg. Perform chiburi to the side, then replace the sword in the scabbard and return to your original position.

JUNTO SONO NI—HOW TO DRAW THE SWORD

1: Step forward with your right foot and grab the *saya* with the left hand.

2: Step forward with the left foot and grab the *tsuka* with the right hand.

3: Step forward with your right foot while performing *nukiuchi* to your opponent's chest.

4: Swing your sword up over your head with your right hand. Your left hand joins your right hand on the tsuka in *furikaburi* while you step forward with your left foot.

CONTINUED ON NEXT PAGE

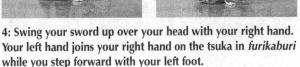

5: Step your right leg forward and cut down at your opponent from overhead. The sword should stop parallel to the ground at waist height.

6: Perform *yoko chiburi*.

7: Push the saya forward to the middle of your body and perform *shoden noto*.

8: Grip the *tsuka gashira* and step your left leg forward to join your right leg in *musubiashi.* Raise your eyes to look at the *shomen.* Until this time, you should have been looking at your fallen opponent.

9: Release your right hand from the tsuka gashira and bring it to the side of your right thigh. Step back, starting with your left leg, in five steps to return to your starting position.

10: Stop and release your left hand from the *koiguchi.* Return to your natural standing posture.

TSUIGEKITO—PURSUING SWORD

While you are walking, the opponent attempts to cut you with a nukitsuke or kirioroshi. To stop his action, you cut toward your opponent's right wrist and chest diagonally. Then, as the opponent moves back, pursue him and cut down at the head of your retreating opponent. Deliver the final cut from overhead with another forward step of your right and left feet.

TSUIGEKITO—HOW TO DRAW THE SWORD

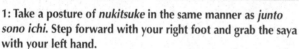
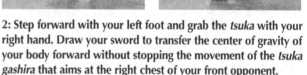

1: Take a posture of *nukitsuke* in the same manner as *junto sono ichi*. Step forward with your right foot and grab the saya with your left hand.

2: Step forward with your left foot and grab the *tsuka* with your right hand. Draw your sword to transfer the center of gravity of your body forward without stopping the movement of the *tsuka gashira* that aims at the right chest of your front opponent.

3: Step forward with your right foot while performing *nukiuchi* to your opponent's chest. Cut diagonally from the right chest to the lower left rib of your opponent while in the power stance. At the moment when you cut, the tsuka gashira is on the line of your waist and your right wrist on the tsuka is aligned with the side of your right knee. The *kissaki* is positioned at the lower left rib of your opponent and on line with your right knee. Your front knee is bent at 110 degrees with your body upright and your rear left knee open and pushing upward.

4: Step your left foot forward to *musubiashi* while pressuring the centerline with the kissaki.

5: Immediately, swing the sword up to cover your left shoulder and over your head. Join your left hand with your right hand on the *tsuka* while stepping your right foot forward in *soeashi* and following it with your left foot.

6: Cut the forehead of your opponent by stepping your right leg forward in *hanzoroe* followed by your left foot. This cut is a *kiritsuke* that stops with the kissaki at face level.

7: Subsequently, step your right foot forward in hanzoroe. Follow it with your left foot, pushing your sword forward and up over your head. Cut down in *kirioroshi* at your opponent from overhead. The tip of the sword finishes on the line of your right knee and parallel to the floor.

8: Step back with the right leg while pushing your sword forward and up to 45 degrees overhead into *jodan no kamae*.

9: Step back with the left leg. Lower your sword downward to take *chudan* or *seigan no kamae*.

10: Perform *yoko chiburi*. The *tsuba* should remain on the same horizontal plane throughout the process in which the kissaki lowers during the *chiburi*.

CONTINUED ON NEXT PAGE

11: Push the saya forward to the middle of your body and perform *shoden noto*.

12: Grip the tsuka gashira and step your left leg forward to join your right leg in *musubiashi*. Raise your eyes to look at the *shomen*. Until this time, you should have been looking at your fallen opponent.

13: Release your right hand from the tsuka gashira and bring it to the side of your right thigh. Step back, starting with your left leg, in five steps to the starting position.

14: Stop and release your left hand from the *koiguchi*. Return to a natural standing posture.

SHATO—ANGULAR SWORD

An opponent to your forward position attempts to cut you. To stop his attack, you directly cut his face and wrists, then cut diagonally down toward the right shoulder of the retreating opponent while stepping forward with your left leg. As the retreating opponent tries to deliver a final cut, move forward with your right foot. Pivot and deliver a diagonal cut through the opponent's body, beginning at his rear left shoulder.

SHATO—HOW TO DRAW THE SWORD

1: Step forward with the right foot and grab the *saya* with the left hand.

2: Step forward with the left foot and grab the *tsuka* with the right hand. Push the sword up toward the opponent's face while turning your body 45 degrees to the left.

3: Step forward with the right foot while performing *nukiuchi* to your opponent's face. The *kissaki* should stop at the height above your right eye.

4: Swing your sword up and over your head with your right hand. The left hand joins your right hand on the tsuka in *furikaburi*.

CONTINUED ON NEXT PAGE

5: Step the left leg forward and cut diagonally down toward your opponent's right shoulder from overhead. The sword should stop just outside your right hip and parallel to the ground at waist height.

6: Raise the sword up to your left on the same line as the previous cut.

7: Step forward to your right and bring the sword overhead. Pivot your hips counterclockwise and cut diagonally toward the back of your opponent's left shoulder.

8: After the sword has made contact, step back with the left foot and allow the sword to continue the cut diagonally to your left hip.

9: Raise the sword back to the centerline in *chudan no kamae.*

10: Perform *yoko chiburi.* The *tsuba* should remain on the same plane as the kissaki drops during *chiburi.*

146

11: Push the *saya* forward to the middle of your body and perform *shoden noto.*

12: Grip the *tsuka-gashira* and step your left leg forward to join your right leg in *musubiashi* and continue to look at the fallen opponent.

CONTINUED ON NEXT PAGE

13: Release your right hand from the tsuka gashira and bring it to the side of your right thigh. Step back starting with your left leg in five steps to the starting position.

14: Stop and release your left hand from the *koiguchi*. Return to a natural standing posture.

SHIHOTO SONO ICHI—FOUR-DIRECTION SWORD NO. 1

Three opponents to your forward left, middle and right positions and one opponent at your rear left corner attempt to cut you. To stop their attack, you threaten to cut the front right-corner enemy with nukitsuke to force him to retreat. Then you thrust to the rear left-corner at the opponent's torso. Cut directly down to your front right-corner opponent. Turn 90 degrees to your left and cut down the left-corner opponent. Turn 45 degrees to the front and cut down the remaining opponent.

SHIHOTO SONO ICHI—HOW TO DRAW THE SWORD

1: Step forward with the right foot and grab the *saya* with the left hand.

2: Step forward with the left foot and grab the *tsuka* with the right hand. Push the sword up toward the right-corner opponent's face while turning your body slightly to the left.

3: Step diagonally to the right while performing *nukiuchi* to your opponent's face; your right leg is forward. The *kissaki* should stop just before it leaves the *koiguchi* with the *tsuka gashira* pointing at the opponent's face.

4: Rotate the sword horizontally into your right hand by turning the saya with your left hand. Open your left hip to release the kissaki from the saya. The saya should be pulled back to form a 90-degree angle to the back of the sword. Thrust the kissaki rearward and down at an angle until the *tsuba* stops under your left breast.

CONTINUED ON NEXT PAGE

5: Reach under and grab the tsuka with your left hand. Swing your sword up overhead with your right and left hand for *furikaburi*. Cut downward toward your right front corner in *kiri-oroshi*. The sword should stop just parallel to the ground at waist height.

6: Rotate your body 90 degrees to your left while turning the sword horizontally toward the left, center and corner opponents.

7: Raise the sword overhead with both hands while stepping forward with your right foot. Step your right foot forward to the left front corner and cut down toward your opponent's head from overhead. The sword should stop parallel to the ground at waist height.

8: Rotate your body 45 degrees to your right while turning the sword blade horizontally toward the right. Face the remaining front-center opponent. Raise the sword overhead with both hands while stepping forward with your right foot. Step with your right foot forward to the front center and cut down toward your opponent's head from overhead. The sword should stop parallel to the ground at waist height.

9: Perform *yoko chiburi*. The kissaki should remain on the same horizontal plane during *chiburi*.

10: Push the *saya* forward to the middle of your body and perform *shoden noto*.

CONTINUED ON NEXT PAGE

11: Grip the tsuka gashira and step your left leg forward to join your right leg in *musubiashi*. Continue to look at the fallen opponent.

12: Release your right hand from the tsuka gashira and bring it to the side of your right thigh. Step back, starting with your left leg, in five steps to your starting position.

13: Stop and release your left hand from the *koiguchi*. Return to a natural standing posture.

SHIHOTO SONO NI—FOUR DIRECTION SWORD NO. 2

Three opponents to your forward left, middle and right positions and one opponent at your rear left corner attempts to cut you. To stop their attack, you threaten to cut the front right-corner enemy with *nukitsuke,* forcing him to retreat. Then you thrust to the rear left-corner opponent's torso. You cut directly down to your front right-corner opponent. As your remaining two opponents retreat, turn 90 degrees to your left and cut down at the left-corner opponent. Turn 45 degrees to the front and cut down the remaining opponent.

SHIHOTO SONO NI—HOW TO DRAW THE SWORD

1: Step forward with the right foot and grab the *saya* with the left hand.

2: Step forward with your left foot and grab the *tsuka* with the right hand. Push the sword up toward the right-corner opponent's face while turning your body slightly to the left.

3: Step to the right diagonally while performing *nukiuchi* to your opponent's face; your right leg is forward. The *kissaki* should stop just before it leaves the *koiguchi* with the *tsuka gashira* pointing at the opponent's face.

4: Rotate the sword horizontally into your right hand by turning the saya with your left hand. Open your left hip to release the kissaki from the saya. The saya should be pulled back to form a 90-degree angle to the back of the sword. Thrust the kissaki rearward and down at an angle until the *tsuba* stops under your left breast.

CONTINUED ON NEXT PAGE

5: Reach under and grab the tsuka with your left hand. Swing your sword up overhead with your right and left hand for *furikaburi*. Cut downward to your right front corner in *kirioroshi*. The sword should stop just parallel to the ground at waist height.

6: Rotate your body 90 degrees to your left while turning the sword horizontally to the left, center and corner opponents.

7: Raise the sword overhead with both hands while stepping forward with your left foot. Step your left foot forward to the left front corner and cut down at your opponent's head. The sword should stop parallel to the ground at waist height.

8: Rotate your body 45 degrees to your right while turning the sword blade horizontally toward the right and facing the remaining front-center opponent. Raise the sword overhead with both hands while stepping forward with your right foot. Step your right foot forward to the front center and cut down at your opponent's head from overhead. The sword should stop parallel to the ground at waist height.

9: Perform *yoko chiburi*. The kissaki should remain on the same horizontal plane during *chiburi*.

10: Push the saya forward to the middle of your body and perform *shoden noto*.

CONTINUED ON NEXT PAGE

11: Grip the tsuka gashira and step your left leg forward to join your right leg in *musubiashi*. Continue to look at the fallen opponent.

12: Release your right hand from the tsuka gashira and bring it to the side of your right thigh. Step back, starting with your left leg, in five steps to return to your starting position.

13: Stop and release your left hand from the *koiguchi*. Return to a natural standing posture.

ZANTOTSUTO—BEHEADING STROKE

While you are walking, the opponent attempts to cut you with a nukitsuke or kirioroshi. To stop his action, you cut diagonally at the opponent's right wrist and chest. Then as the opponent moves back, pursue him and thrust toward his throat. Continue to push him back before delivering the final cut from overhead with another forward step of your right and left foot.

ZANTOTSUTO—HOW TO DRAW THE SWORD

1: Take a posture of *nukitsuke* in the same manner as *tsuigekito*. Step forward with the right foot and grab the *saya* with the left hand.

2: Step forward with the left foot and grab the *tsuka* with the right hand. Draw your sword to transfer the center of gravity forward without stopping the movement of the *tsuka gashira*, which is aiming at the right chest of your front opponent.

3: Step forward with the right foot while performing *nukiuchi* to your opponent's chest. Cut diagonally from the right chest to the left lower rib of your opponent while in the power stance. At the moment when you cut, the *gashira* is on the line of your waist, and your right wrist on the tsuka is aligned with the side of your right knee. The *kissaki* is positioned at your opponent's lower left rib and on the line of your right knee. Your front knee is bent 110 degrees with your body upright and your rear left knee open and pushing upward.

CONTINUED ON NEXT PAGE

4: Step left foot forward to *musubiashi* while pressuring the center line with the kissaki.

5: Step forward with the right foot and thrust the kissaki to the opponent's throat. The kissaki should stop at the height of your own forehead. Your body should be slightly inclined forward as you complete the thrusting action.

6: Withdraw the sword while you step forward with the left foot in to musubi-ashi while maintaining pressure on the centerline.

7: Immediately swing the sword up overhead while stepping forward with the right foot and cutting downward to the opponent's head in *kirioroshi*.

8: Perform *yoko chiburi*. The *tsuba* should remain on the same horizontal plane throughout this process while the kissaki lowers during *chiburi*.

9: Push the saya forward to the middle of your body and perform *shoden noto*.

10: Grip the tsuka gashira and step your left leg forward to join your right leg in musubiashi. Raise your eyes to look at the *shomen*. Until this time, you should have been looking at the fallen opponent.

CONTINUED ON NEXT PAGE

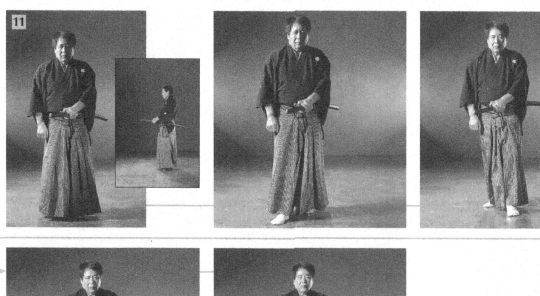

11: Release your right hand from the tsuka gashira and bring it to the side of your right thigh. Step back, starting with your left leg, in five steps to the starting position.

12: Stop and release your left hand from the *koiguchi*.
Return to a natural standing posture.

ZENTEKIGYAKUTO SONO ICHI (O KU IAI)

While you are walking, the front opponent attempts to cut you. In anticipation of his drawing action, you cut upward and diagonally from the opponent's right abdomen to his shoulder *(gyaku kesa-giri)*. Continue to step forward and cut diagonally down through his right shoulder to his hip (kesa-giri).

ZENTEKIGYAKUTO SONO ICHI—HOW TO DRAW THE SWORD

1: Step forward with the right foot followed by the left foot while walking naturally with hands at your sides.

2: At the second or fourth step with the left leg forward, simultaneously grasp the mouth of the *saya* with the left hand and the *tsuka* with the right hand. Perform *okuden koiguchi no kiri kata.*

3: Step forward with the right foot while performing a rising cut to the opponent's chest and raised arms. This cut is performed while the hips turn clockwise in the *Tanimura-ha* tradition. Draw the sword horizontally with the right hand to as far as the *kissaki* toward the center of the opponent's abdomen. Pull the saya back with the left hand while transferring your center of gravity forward with a push forward of your right shoulder. In the finishing position of this cut, the sword continues to travel outward and into *furikaburi*—outside of the body and into a cutting position above the head.

CONTINUED ON NEXT PAGE

4: As you swing the sword up overhead with the right hand, join the left hand with the right hand on the tsuka for furika-buri.

5: Continue to step forward with your left foot and cut down diagonally from the opponent's right shoulder to his left abdomen. Perform this cut in the *okuden* style of *kirioroshi* by opening the right hip at the moment of impact with the target. At the end of the cut down, the *tsuka gashira* is positioned one-grip space in front of the right side of your navel and the kissaki is in line with your right knee. The sword should stop parallel to the ground at waist height on the line of the right hip

6: Return the kissaki to the position of *seigan* while facing the centerline.

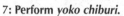

7: Perform *yoko chiburi*.

8: Push the saya forward to the middle of the body and perform *okuden noto*.

9: Grip the tsuka gashira and step the right leg forward to join the left leg in *musubiashi*. Raise your eyes to look at the *shomen*. Until this time, you should have been looking at the fallen opponent.

10: Continue to hold the right hand on the tsuka gashira. Step back starting with the left leg in five steps to the starting position.

CONTINUED ON NEXT PAGE

11: Stop and release the right hand then the left hand from the *koiguchi*. Return to a natural standing posture.

ZENTEKIGYAKUTO SONO NI (OKU IAI)

While you are walking, the front opponent attempts to cut you. In anticipation of his drawing action, you cut upward and diagonally from the right abdomen to the shoulder of your opponent (gyaku kesa-giri). Then cut down through his left shoulder diagonally to his hip (kesa-giri).

ZENTEKIGYAKUTO SONO NI—HOW TO DRAW THE SWORD

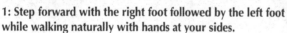

1: Step forward with the right foot followed by the left foot while walking naturally with hands at your sides.

2: At the second or fourth step with the left leg forward, simultaneously grasp the mouth of the *saya* with the left hand and the *tsuka* with the right hand to perform *okuden koiguchi no kiri kata*.

3: Step forward with the right foot while performing a rising cut to the opponent's chest and raised arms. This cut is performed while the hips turn counterclockwise in the *Shimomura-ha* tradition. Draw the sword horizontally with the right hand to as far as the kissaki toward the center of the opponent's abdomen. Pull the saya back with the left hand while transferring your center of gravity forward with a push forward of your right shoulder. In the finishing position of this cut, the sword stops upward at a 45-degree angle from the right shoulder. The kissaki stops forward and parallel to the ground.

4: Step forward with the left foot. Swing the sword up overhead with the right hand. Join the left hand with the right hand on the tsuka (*furikaburi*).

5: Continue to step forward with your right foot and cut down diagonally from the opponent's left shoulder to his right abdomen. Perform this cut in the *okuden* style of *kirioroshi* by opening the left hip at the moment of impact with the target. At the end of the downward cut, the *gashira* is positioned at one-grip space in front of the left side of your navel and the kissaki is in line with your left knee. The sword should stop parallel to the ground at waist height on the line of the left hip.

6: Return the kissaki to the position of *seigan* while facing the centerline.

CONTINUED ON NEXT PAGE

7: Perform *yoko chiburi.*

8: Push the *saya* forward to the middle of the body and perform *okuden noto.*

9: Grip the *tsuka gashira* and step the left leg forward to join the right leg in *musubiashi*. Raise your eyes to look at the *shomen*. Until this time, you should have been looking at the fallen opponent.

10: Continue to hold the right hand on the tsuka gashira. Step back, starting with the left leg, in five steps to your starting position.

11: Stop and release the right hand and then the left hand from the *koiguchi*. Return to a natural standing posture.

TATEKITO (OKU IAI)

Two opponents are in forward diagonal-left and diagonal-right positions. There is also one opponent at the rear left corner. You are unsure if there might be others. When they attempt to attack or converge on you, threaten to cut the front right-corner enemy with nukitsuke, forcing him to retreat. Then thrust into the enemy's torso that is positioned to the rear left corner. Continue to turn and cut directly down at the head of the retreating enemy to the front right corner. Pursue the final opponent by turning 90 degrees to the left. Step forward and cut him down. Continue to anticipate another attack that does not materialize. End by performing yoko chiburi and noto.

TATEKITO—HOW TO DRAW THE SWORD

1: Step forward with the right foot. Your hands should be hanging naturally to your sides.

2: Step forward with the left foot and grab the *tsuka* and *saya* with both hands while performing *okuden koiguchi no kiri kata*. Push the sword up toward the right-corner opponent's face while turning your body slightly to the left.

3: Step diagonally to the right while performing *nuki-uchi* to your opponent's face; your right leg is forward. The *kissaki* should stop just before it leaves the *koiguchi* with the *tsuka gashira* pointing at the opponent's face.

4: Rotate the sword horizontally into the right hand by turning the saya with the left hand. Rotate your left hip counterclockwise to release the kissaki from the saya. The saya should be pulled back to form a 90-degree angle to the back of the sword. Thrust the kissaki rearward and down at an angle until the *tsuba* stops under the left breast.

5: Reach under and grab the tsuba with your left hand. Swing your sword up overhead with the right hand and left hand for *furikaburi*. Cut downward toward the opponent's head, which is positioned to the right front corner, in *kirioroshi*. The sword should stop parallel to the ground at waist height.

6: Rotate your body 90 degrees to the left while turning the sword horizontally toward the left, center and corner opponents.

7: Raise the sword overhead with both hands while stepping forward with your left foot. Step the left foot forward to the left front corner and cut down at the opponent's head. The sword should stop parallel to the ground at waist height. Continue to maintain a lingering awareness for a fourth attacker that does not materialize.

8: Perform *yoko chiburi*. The kissaki should remain on the same horizontal plane during *chiburi*.

CONTINUED ON NEXT PAGE

9: Push the saya forward to the middle of the body and perform *okuden noto*.

10: Grip the tsuka gashira and step your right leg forward to join your left leg in *musubiashi*. Continue to look at the fallen opponent.

11: Continue to hold the right hand on the tsuka gashira. Step back, starting with the left leg, in five steps to return to the starting position.

12: Stop and release the right hand from the *koiguchi* followed by the left hand. Return to a natural standing posture.

KOTEKIGYAKUTO (OKU IAI)

Two opponents are walking in front of and behind you. The rear opponent attempts to cut you. In advance of his action, you turn around and cut upward from his right abdomen to the left shoulder in gyaku kesa-giri. For the front opponent, cut down from the left shoulder diagonally in kesa-giri.

KOTEKIGYAKUTO—HOW TO DRAW THE SWORD

1: Step forward with the right foot followed by the left foot while walking naturally with hands at your sides.

CONTINUED ON NEXT PAGE

2: At the third or fifth step with the right leg forward, simultaneously grasp the mouth of the *saya* with the left hand and the *tsuka* with the right hand to perform *okuden koiguchi no kiri kata*. This step should be slightly to the left, crossing in front of your centerline.

3: As you turn counterclockwise with your hips and your right leg forward, turn toward the left on your right heel to face the rear opponent. Draw your sword up to the *kissaki*.

4: As soon as you face the rear opponent, reverse the saya and cut upward from his right abdomen to the left shoulder, pulling the *saya* back with your left hand in *gyaku kesa-giri*. At this moment, the right hand is positioned to 45 degrees right outside your body and 45 degrees up on the line of your right shoulder. The sword is toward the front and is parallel with the ground. The blade is inclined upward at 45 degrees. This *nukitsuke* can be performed in the *Shimomura-ha* or *Tanimura-ha* tradition, depending on the distance and timing of the attacker.

5: Immediately, turn clockwise on your left heel to the right to face the front opponent. When turning, swing your sword up overhead, covering your left shoulder, and join your left hand with your right hand on the tsuka. In one motion, cut downward and diagonally from the left shoulder to the right trunk of the front opponent in *okuden kirioroshi*. At this moment, the kissaki is before your left knee and the *gashira* is positioned in one-grip space before the right side of your navel.

6: Return the kissaki to the position of *seigan* while facing the centerline.

7: Perform *yoko chiburi*.

8: Push the saya forward to the middle of the body and perform *okuden noto*.

CONTINUED ON NEXT PAGE

9: Grip the *tsuka gashira* and step the right leg forward to join the left leg in *musubiashi*. Raise your eyes to look at the *shomen*. Until this time, you should have been looking at the fallen opponent.

10: Continue to hold the right hand on the tsuka gashira. Step back, starting with the left leg, in five steps to return to your starting position.

11: Stop and release the right hand and then the left hand from the *koiguchi*. Return to a natural standing posture.

KOTEKINUKIUCHI (OKU IAI)

Two opponents are walking in front of and behind you. The rear opponent attempts to cut you. In advance of his action, you turn around in a clockwise motion and cut down and diagonally through the opponent's right shoulder in kesa-giri. You then turn counterclockwise and cut down and diagonally toward the front opponent's right shoulder in *okuden kesa-giri*. Finish by performing yoko chiburi and okuden noto.

KOTEKINUKIUCHI—HOW TO DRAW THE SWORD

1: Step forward with the right foot followed by the left foot while walking naturally with hands at your sides.

2: At the second or fourth step with the left leg forward, simultaneously grasp the mouth of the *saya* with the left hand and *tsuka* with the right hand to perform *okuden koiguchi no kiri kata*. This step should be slightly toward the right crossing in front of your centerline.

3: As you turn clockwise with your hips and left leg forward, turn toward the right on your left heel to face the rear opponent. Draw your sword up to the *kissaki*.

4: As you turn around from the right to face the rear opponent, cut downward and diagonally from his right shoulder until the tip of the sword comes to before your right knee in the posture of *hanmi*. The kissaki should continue to press toward the opponent's left hip and ribs. This *nukitsuke* can be performed in the *Shimomura-ha* or *Tanimura-ha* tradition, depending on the distance and timing of the attacker.

CONTINUED ON NEXT PAGE

5: Immediately, turn counterclockwise on your right heel to face the front opponent. At the same time, grasp the tsuka with the left hand and transition through *waki no kamae*, raising the sword up overhead to cover your right shoulder. Instantly, when you face the front opponent, perform *kesa-giri* in *okuden* fashion: downward and diagonally from the opponent's right shoulder to his left hip in the posture of hanmi. At this moment, the kissaki is before your right knee and parallel to the floor. The *gashira* is positioned in one-grip space before the left side of your navel, which is the centerline in the posture of hanmi.

6: Return the kissaki to the position of *seigan* while facing the centerline.

7: Perform *yoko chiburi*.

8: Push the saya forward to the middle of the body and perform *okuden noto*.

9: Grip the *tsuka gashira* and step the right leg forward to join the left leg in *musubiashi*. Raise your eyes to look at the *shomen*. Until this time, you should have been looking at the fallen opponent.

CONTINUED ON NEXT PAGE

10: Continue to hold the right hand on the tsuka gashira. Step back, starting with the left leg, in five steps to return to your starting position.

11: Stop and release the right hand and then the left hand from the *koiguchi.* Return to a natural standing posture.

CHAPTER 8

KUMITACHI—PAIRED FENCING

You may ask why there should be an emphasis on kenjutsu kumitachi practices within the modern day practice of Japanese sword arts. The answer is quite simple: The study of the sword is the study of face-to-face combat—the study of life and death. It therefore stands to reason that in order to truly understand the sword arts, it's necessary to engage in the regular practice of kumitachi (also known as katachi), which are the paired waza of kenjutsu and battojutsu. However, most practitioners of the Japanese sword arts today focus only on *batto waza* and engage in little if any paired practice. This is a mistake that results in an incomplete understanding of how to truly use the sword—how to really express the true depth and breadth of the battojutsu and kenjutsu.

A training partner changes the feeling and understanding of everything in a practitioner's swordsmanship—timing, footwork, distancing and the feeling of receiving a real attack to name just a few. An excellent example of this difference is in the correct use of the shinogi. There are many battojutsu schools that really do not seem to know how to use the shinogi when receiving an attack from a training partner. But through paired *bokken* (wooden sword) practice, you can learn how to deflect and kill the power of a partner's attack. In fact, the bokken provides excellent feedback with respect to a properly executed technique. When receiving an attack, the proper use of the shinogi of the bokken will result in a sharp "clack" rather than a dull thud. Hasuji also can change dramatically from solo batto waza to paired practice. Hasuji that may seem effortless in batto waza may be greatly affected by an opponent's effort to counter your technique in kumitachi.

Breathing is another element in your practice that may change dramatically when engaged in the rigorous practice of kumitachi. While you can learn to regulate your breath control through *batto waza*, the nature of solo training allows you to do so at your own pace. The pressure of a live opponent in kumitachi forces the practitioner to learn to apply that same control through the crucible of committed paired practice.

Throughout the history of Eishin-ryu, some form of prearranged kumitachi with bokken to facilitate safe practice with a partner has been practiced. It was meant to be the general curriculum's substitute for using a *shinken* (live sword). Early forms of Eishin-ryu kumitachi were likely single encounters that allowed the sword student to develop basic responses to a particular attack. Throughout the ages, various martial strategies evolved and were likely incorporated and expanded on within the basic kumitachi.

The kumitachi in this chapter are a representation of older battojutsu and kenjutsu forms of the *Eishin-ryu batto-ho iai kumitachi.* In each kumitachi, one partner demonstrates a key principle of battojutsu while the other partner enacts the appropriate offensive and defensive responses. The koryu method for teaching these kumitachi traditionally places the senior partner playing the uchitachi to his junior counterpart, who plays the shitachi. Shitachi's role is to enact the inherent principle being practiced. Uchitachi assists shitachi in carrying out his role as the victor. This does not suggest that uchitachi plays a passive role. On the contrary, uchitachi must continue to pressure his partner to perform precisely and accurately for each attack or counterattack. As the shitachi continues to make progress in his study, the uchitachi makes the timing, distancing and other tactics more challenging. Therefore, it is the role of uchitachi to lose each battle by a small margin while shitachi continues to push the limits of his own ability. Winning is easy, but losing by the same small margin while the opponent improves his skill is extremely difficult to understand and master.

Before performing the actual kumitachi sets, both partners should perform the preparation and etiquette as prescribed in earlier chapters. Proper respect should be paid to the training area, bokken and each partner before commencing. These ritual acts set the stage and proper attitude for training. The act of conscious preparation instills in the swordsman the sincerity and humility that is necessary for cooperating with his colleague in a role that necessitates self-sacrifice for the good of his training partner.

The general principles presented in Chapter Four should be given special consideration while carrying out the roles of shitachi and uchitachi. Progress can only be achieved by embracing the principles of eye contact, breath control, pressure, timing, distancing and awareness. As a deeper understanding of the underlying principles of each waza reveal themselves, the flavor of the kumitachi becomes palpable to even a casual observer. This is the flavor of one's *fukaku*, which is the depth of character and understanding that seasons each movement and brings life to the kumitachi.

The Six Kumitachi of Eishin-Ryu Batto-Ho Iai Kumitachi
Deai—First Meeting
Ukenagashi—Flowing Block
Tsukikage—Moon Shadow
Suigetsuto—Solar-Plexus Thrust
Dokumyoken—Miraculous Sword
Tsubamegaeshi—Turning Swallow

The sequences of kumitachi as presented in this chapter start and end closer than they would normally be performed. The photography was shot in an enclosed environment and prohibited the necessary space for these kumitachi to be depicted at the normal distances. Each of these sets should begin and end with uchitachi and shitachi at approximately ten paces from one another.

DEAI—FIRST MEETING

While you are walking, an opponent to your forward position attempts to draw and cut you in a downward kesa-giri. To stop his attack, you perform an upward nukitsuke from left to right and block the attack to your neck. Following the opponent's retreat and as he attempts to thrust to your solar plexus, move to the side and cut his neck with a kesa-giri. The swordsmen return to a chudan no kamae position and then lower the swords to gedan no kamae. Both swordsmen return to the original starting positions.

DEAI—HOW TO DRAW THE SWORD

1: Uchitachi: Step forward with the left foot and grab the sword with the left and right hand. Draw the sword forward toward your opponent's center. Step forward with the right foot and perform a downward left to right cut toward his neck.

Shitachi: Step forward with your left foot and grab the sword with the left and right hand. Draw the sword forward toward the center of *uchitachi*. Step back with the left foot and perform an upward left-to-right cut to block uchitachi's sword.

2: Uchitachi: As you feel *shitachi* pressure you with his sword, step back with the right foot and assume *chudan no kasumi*. Maintain control of the centerline with the *kissaki*.

Shitachi: As you feel uchitachi release the pressure on your sword, step back with the right foot into *jodan no kamae*.

CONTINUED ON NEXT PAGE

3: Uchitachi: Shuffle forward with your leading left foot while maintaining chudan no kasumi. Cross-step forward with the right foot while threatening the centerline with the kissaki. Step forward quickly with the left then right foot while performing an upward thrust to your opponent's chest and throat. End with your right leg forward.

Shitachi: Maintain jodan no kamae until uchitachi attempts to thrust through the centerline. As uchitachi thrusts, step forward in *irimi-tenshin* with the right foot to the right front corner and perform a downward *kesa-giri* to uchitachi's neck.

4: Uchitachi: Lower the sword to knee level and shuffle back with the left foot followed by the right foot. As shitachi regains a position on line in *chudan no kamae*, raise the sword to match his chudan no kamae position. The swords should cross on the left side of the blades.

Shitachi: As uchitachi lowers the sword to *gedan no kamae* and shuffles back, maintain pressure on his throat with the kissaki. Also move back on the line of attack by shifting the left then right foot into position. Maintain pressure while uchitachi raises his sword to chudan no kamae.

5: Uchitachi: Turn the cutting edge of the sword inward toward shitachi's blade. Lower the sword simultaneously with shitachi into gedan no kamae while maintaining a connection to his sword along the cutting edge. Shuffle back with your left then right foot. Release the connection to shitachi's sword at the kissaki when you separate. Return to your original starting position by taking three or five steps back while maintaining gedan no kamae.

Shitachi: Turn the cutting edge of the sword inward toward uchitachi's blade. Lower the sword simultaneously with uchitachi into gedan no kamae while maintaining a connection to his sword along the cutting edge. Shuffle back with your left then right foot. Release the connection to uchitachi's sword at the kissaki when you separate. Return to your original starting position by taking three or five steps back while maintaining gedan no kamae.

UKENAGASHI—FLOWING BLOCK

While you are walking, an opponent to your forward position performs a draw and cut to your neck with a horizontal nukitsuke. To negate his cut, you perform a nukitsuke from left to right while rotating the sword vertically and block the oncoming attack. Subsequent to his failed first attack and retreat, the opponent attempts a second cut to the left side of your neck. You receive and stop his oncoming attack by retreating and performing kiritsuke. As you pressure the opponent to retreat a second time, perform a cut to the right side of his neck. When the opponent blocks your attack, you attempt to cut through his right wrist with a downward stroke. To avoid getting cut, the opponent retreats into jodan no kamae. As he performs a final cut to your head, perform an upward flowing block while moving to the side and cutting his head in kirioroshi. Both swordsmen return to a chudan no kamae position and lower the swords to gedan no kamae. You end the kumitachi by returning to the original starting positions.

UKENAGASHI—HOW TO DRAW THE SWORD

1: Uchitachi: Step forward with the left foot and grab the sword with the left and right hand. Draw the sword forward toward your opponent's center. Step forward with the right foot and perform a horizontal left-to-right *nukitsuke* cut toward his neck.

Shitachi: Step forward with the left foot and grab the sword with the left and right hand. Draw the sword forward toward uchitachi and control his center. Step back with the left foot and perform a left-to-right cut while rotating the blade vertically to block his sword.

2: Uchitachi: As you feel *shitachi* pressure the block, step back with the right foot and assume *hasso no kamae*.

Shitachi: When you feel uchitachi release the pressure on your sword, step back with the right foot into hasso no kamae.

3: Uchitachi: Shuffle forward with your leading left foot while maintaining hasso no kamae. Step forward with the right foot and raise the sword into *jodan* as your right foot passes your left foot. Step forward quickly with the right foot and perform a right-to-left *kesa-giri* to shitachi's neck. End with your right leg forward.

Shitachi: Shuffle backward with your rear right foot while maintaining hasso no kamae. Step backward with the left foot and raise the sword into jodan as your left foot passes your right foot. Step back quickly with the left foot and perform a right-to-left *kiritsuke* to block uchitachi's oncoming attack. End with your right leg forward. Take control of the centerline with the *kissaki* while you perform the kiritsuke. The finishing position prevents uchitachi from thrusting to your center.

4: Uchitachi: As shitachi thrusts forward with the kissaki, shuffle backward with your left foot. Then step backward with the right foot and raise the sword into jodan as your right foot passes your left foot. Step back quickly with the right foot and perform a left-to-right kiritsuke to block shitachi's oncoming attack. End with your left leg forward. Take control of the centerline with the kissaki as you perform the kiritsuke. The finishing position stops shitachi's forward momentum. The swords are now crossed at the *ura* position on their right sides.

Shitachi: Once you have stopped uchitachi's oncoming attack, shuffle forward with your leading right foot while maintaining pressure on the centerline. Step forward with the left foot and raise the sword into jodan as your left foot passes your right foot. Step forward quickly with the left foot and perform a left-to-right kesa-giri to uchitachi's neck, ending with your left leg forward. As uchitachi blocks your attack, the swords will be crossed on their left sides.

5: Uchitachi: As shitachi attempts to cut your exposed right wrist, shuffle back with your right foot into *jodan no kamae*.

Shitachi: Rotate your hips counterclockwise and attempt to cut uchitachi's right wrist. When uchitachi retreats to jodan no kamae, assume *chudan no kamae* and slowly lower the kissaki clockwise to your right front corner.

CONTINUED ON NEXT PAGE

6: Uchitachi: When shitachi lowers his kissaki toward your left side, step forward with the right foot and cut fully downward from his head to his hips in a downward *kirioroshi*.

Shitachi: As uchitachi begins the cut to your head, raise the sword upward and make contact with the opponent's sword on the left side of your blade at the *shinogi*. Maintain blade contact while you slide your left foot diagonally forward in a *tenshin* movement to the left front corner. As you step, duck under your sword when it is receiving uchitachi's sword attack. Allow your own blade to be pushed and swung to the right by uchitachi's cut while you cover your head and right shoulder with your own sword. Release uchitachi's blade on the right side and move left and past his downward cut to your right side. With your left foot forward, deliver a kirioroshi to the right side of uchitachi's head in one fluid motion.

7: Uchitachi: Shuffle your left foot back then move your sword under shitachi's sword. Raise the sword to meet shitachi's sword in *chudan no kamae*.

Shitachi: As *uchitachi* shuffles back, step the right foot back on line followed by stepping the left foot back. Lower the sword into chudan no kamae.

8: Uchitachi: Turn the cutting edge of the sword inward toward shitachi's blade. Lower the sword simultaneously with shitachi into *gedan no kamae* while maintaining a connection to his sword along the cutting edge. Shuffle back with your left and then right foot. Release the connection to shitachi's sword at the kissaki as you both separate. Return to your original starting position by taking three or five steps back while maintaining gedan no kamae.

Shitachi: Turn the cutting edge of the sword inward toward uchitachi's blade. Lower the sword simultaneously with uchitachi into gedan no kamae while maintaining a connection to his sword along the cutting edge. Shuffle back with your left and then right foot. Release the connection to uchitachi's sword at the kissaki as you both separate. Return to your starting original position by taking three or five steps back while maintaining gedan no kamae.

TSUKIKAGE—MOON SHADOW

While you are walking, an opponent to your forward position attempts to cut you in a downward kirioroshi. To stop his attack, you perform an upward block from gedan no kamae and receive his sword's energy by drawing the attack forward to the left side of your head. As the opponent recovers by dropping his elbows downward and while moving his body forward, you lower your sword and meet him in a crossed-sword position *(tsubazeriai)*. When neither of you find an opening in your opponent's defenses, you push apart and separate into waki no kamae. As the opponent attempts to cut to your body, shuffle back to avoid his attack by moving through jodan no kamae and cut to his head in kirioroshi. The swordsmen return to a chudan no kamae position and then lower the swords to gedan no kamae. Both swordsmen return to the original starting positions.

TSUKIKAGE—HOW TO DRAW THE SWORD

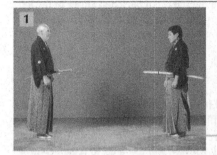

1: Uchitachi: Step forward with the right foot and draw the sword into *chudan no kamae.*

Shitachi: Step forward with the right foot and draw the sword into chudan no kamae.

2: Uchitachi: Step with the left foot forward to *jodan no kamae.*

Shitachi: Lower the sword to *gedan no kamae.*

CONTINUED ON NEXT PAGE

3: Uchitachi: Shuffle forward with your leading left foot while maintaining jodan no kamae. Step forward quickly with the right foot while performing a downward cut to your opponent's head.

Shitachi: Maintain gedan no kamae until uchitachi attempts to cut to the head. Slide the right foot back and closer to the left foot while performing an upward rising block from gedan no kamae. Receive the energy of uchitachi's sword by raising the hips and drawing the attack toward the left side of your head. Your hands should be on the left side of the body and your *kissaki* pointing toward the right front corner.

4: Uchitachi: After the energy of the cut is absorbed when *shitachi* blocks, shuffle forward with the right foot followed by the left foot. As you move forward, lower your center and move your elbows downward while you try to regain control of the combative space. The hand guard *(tsuba)* of your sword will meet the hand guard of shitachi's sword in crossed position in front of the body *(tsubazeriai)*.

Shitachi: As uchitachi attempts to move forward to regain control, lower your center and move your elbows downward to maintain control of the combative space. The hand guard of your sword will meet the hand guard of uchitachi's sword in a crossed position in front of the body. Try to maintain the upper position on top of uchitachi's tsuba.

5: Uchitachi: Try to find the opening *(suki)* in shitachi's position while maintaining a position of defense that does not reveal your intentions. When you are satisfied that no opening exists, separate from shitachi by shuffling back with the left foot while maintaining pressure against his sword. When the distance is correct, push off of his sword in order to raise your sword through *jodan* as you step back with the right foot to *waki no kamae.*

Shitachi: Try to find the opening in uchitachi's position while maintaining a position of defense that does not reveal your intentions. When you are satisfied that no opening exists, separate from him by shuffling back with the left foot and while maintaining pressure against his sword. When the distance is correct, push off of his sword in order to raise your sword through jodan as you step back with your right foot to waki no kamae.

Note to Uchitachi and Shitachi: The position of tsubazeriai offers many options for both swordsmen. Each is searching for an opportunity to cut his adversary while cloaking his own intentions. It is critical to maintain a balanced power and light grip so as not to communicate to the opponent where the attack is strong or weak. The opponent's position may be exploited by moving forward, backward or to either side of the attacking energy. Continued study with a partner is critical to a full understanding of this position.

6: Uchitachi: Shuffle forward with the left foot. Step the right foot forward and perform a right-to-left horizontal cut completely across shitachi's body.

Shitachi: When uchitachi shuffles forward with the left foot, match his movement by shuffling back with the right foot and push energy downward and behind you into the kissaki. As uchitachi steps forward with the right foot and cuts across the body, step the left foot back to a parallel position to the right foot and continue to swing the sword above the head in jodan. Step forward with the right foot as uchitachi's sword passes your right hip. Cut downward in *kirioroshi* to his head.

Note to Uchitachi and Shitachi: Your swords should complete their movements at the exact same time.

CONTINUED ON NEXT PAGE

7: Uchitachi: Lower the sword to knee level and shuffle step back with the left foot followed by the right foot. As shitachi regains a position on line in chudan no kamae, raise the sword to chudan no kamae, also. The swords should cross on the left side of the blades.

Shitachi: As uchitachi lowers the sword to gedan no kamae and shuffles back, exert pressure on his centerline with the kissaki. Maintain pressure as uchitachi raises his sword to chudan no kamae.

8: Uchitachi: Turn the cutting edge of the sword inward toward shitachi's blade. Lower the sword simultaneously with shitachi into gedan no kamae while maintaining a connection to his sword along the cutting edge. Shuffle back with your left and then right foot. Release the connection to shitachi's sword at the kissaki as you both separate. Return to your original starting position by taking three or five steps back while maintaining gedan no kamae.

Shitachi: Turn the cutting edge of the sword inward toward uchitachi's blade. Lower the sword simultaneously with uchitachi into gedan no kamae while maintaining a connection to his sword along the cutting edge. Shuffle back with your left and then right foot. Release the connection to shitachi's sword at the kissaki as you both separate. Return to your starting original position by taking three or five steps back while maintaining gedan no kamae.

SUIGETSUTO—SOLAR-PLEXUS THRUST

While you are walking, an opponent to your forward position attempts to cut you in a downward kesa. You receive and stop his oncoming attack by retreating and performing kiritsuke. As you pressure the opponent to retreat, perform a cut to the right side of his neck. When he blocks the attack, you continue to force him backward and follow up with a kesa-giri cut to the left side of his head. As the opponent blocks this attack and recovers, you lower your sword and meet him in a chudan no kamae. While he attempts to thrust to your solar plexus, push his sword upward with a sliding block as you move to your left front corner and cut him down with kirioroshi. The swordsmen return to a chudan no kamae position and then lower the swords to gedan no kamae. Both swordsmen return to the original starting positions.

SUIGETSUTO—HOW TO DRAW THE SWORD

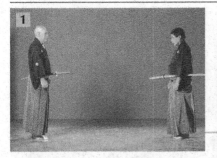  

1: Uchitachi: Step forward with the right foot and draw the sword into *chudan no kamae*. Step with the left foot forward into *hasso no kamae.*

Shitachi: Step forward with the right foot and draw the sword into chudan no kamae. Step back with the right foot into hasso no kamae.

2: Uchitachi: Step forward with the left foot then right foot, alternating until you are within cutting distance of *shitachi*. Shuffle the left foot forward a step followed by a step with the right foot forward and cut to shitachi's head.

Shitachi: As *uchitachi* attempts to cut, shuffle the right foot back then step back in *ayumi-ashi* with the left foot and perform a downward right-to-left cut to block uchitachi's sword and control the centerline of the attack.

Note to Uchitachi and Shitachi: All cuts should be performed from a *jodan* position. Both combatants transition through jodan as their feet pass each other while stepping in ayumi-ashi.

CONTINUED ON NEXT PAGE

3: Uchitachi: Shuffle the left foot back while shitachi pressures your centerline. Step the right foot back and cut downward from left to right to block shitachi's cut to your head.

Shitachi: Shuffle forward with your right foot to pressure uchitachi to move back. Step forward quickly with the left foot while performing a downward cut to uchitachi's right. Maintain control of the centerline with the *kissaki* at the end of the cut.

4: Uchitachi: Shuffle the right foot back again when shitachi pressures your centerline. Step the left foot back and cut downward from right to left to block shitachi's cut to your head. Try to regain control of the centerline with the kissaki as you perform this cut.

Shitachi: Shuffle forward with your left foot to pressure uchitachi to move back. Step forward quickly with the right foot while performing a downward cut to uchitachi's left. Try to maintain control of the centerline with the kissaki at the end of the cut.

Note to Uchitachi and Shitachi: The end position of this cut leaves both uchitachi's and shitachi's kissaki just off of the centerline.

5: Uchitachi: After the energy of shitachi's cut has been absorbed by your block, shuffle backward with the left foot followed by the right foot. As you move back, lower your elbows downward while you try to regain control of the combative space. Match shitachi's sword in chudan no kamae.

Shitachi: As uchitachi stops your forward momentum, attempt to regain control of the centerline. Shuffle back with the left foot followed by the right foot and move your elbows downward while you attempt to maintain control of the combative space. Match uchitachi's sword in chudan no kamae.

6: Uchitachi: Try to find the opening *(suki)* in shitachi's position while maintaining a position of defense that does not reveal your intentions. When you are satisfied that the centerline is open, immediately shuffle forward with the right foot and thrust to shitachi's solar plexus. As shitachi moves forward, continue to thrust upward.

Shitachi: Try to find the opening (suki) in uchitachi's position while maintaining a position of defense that does not reveal your intentions. When uchitachi thrusts to your solar plexus, push his sword upward with the left side of your sword. You use a sliding block as you move your left and right foot off line to the left front corner. Cut down with *kirioroshi* to uchitachi's head.

7: Uchitachi: Lower the sword to knee level and shuffle step back with the left foot followed by the right foot. While shitachi regains a position on line in chudan no kamae, raise the sword to chudan no kamae. The swords should cross on the left side of each blade.

Shitachi: As uchitachi lowers the sword to gedan then shuffles back, exert pressure on his centerline with the kissaki. Maintain pressure when uchitachi raises his sword to chudan no kamae.

8: Uchitachi: Turn the cutting edge of the sword inward toward shitachi's blade. Lower the sword simultaneously with shitachi into *gedan no kamae* while maintaining a connection to his sword along the cutting edge. Shuffle back with your left foot a step and then your right foot. Release the connection to shitachi's sword at the kissaki as you both separate. Return to your original starting position by taking three or five steps back while maintaining gedan no kamae.

Shitachi: Turn the cutting edge of the sword inward toward uchitachi's blade. Lower the sword simultaneously with uchitachi into gedan no kamae while maintaining a connection to his sword along the cutting edge. Shuffle back a step with your left foot then right foot. Release the connection to uchitachi's sword at the kissaki as you both separate. Return to your starting original position by taking three or five steps back while maintaining gedan no kamae.

DOKUMYOKEN—MIRACULOUS SWORD

While you are walking, an opponent to your forward position attempts to cut you in a downward kesa-giri. You receive and stop his oncoming kesa cut by retreating and performing a kiritsuke. His attack controls the centerline, and he immediately launches into a second kesa cut to the opposite side. Your second kiritsuke stops his attack but fails to regain control of the centerline. As the enemy advances and attempts to make a third cut to the center of your head, you shorten the distance as you retreat and use the sword to block directly overhead while using both hands. From an overhead block, you perform a pushing block *(suriuke)* that deflects his sword to the right front corner. As you pressure the opponent to retreat, perform a thrust to the right side of his body at the rib cage. As the opponent continues to retreat into chudan no kamae while moving his body back, you raise your sword and meet him in a chudan no kamae. The swordsmen then lower their swords to gedan no kamae. Both swordsmen return to the original starting positions.

DOKUMYOKEN—HOW TO DRAW THE SWORD

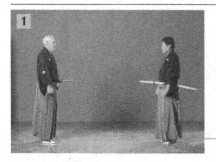  

1: Uchitachi: Step forward with the right foot and draw the sword into *chudan no kamae*. Step forward with the left foot into *hasso no kamae.*

Shitachi: Step forward with the right foot and draw the sword into chudan no kamae. Step back with the right foot into hasso no kamae.

2: Uchitachi: Step forward with the left foot then right foot, alternating until within cutting distance of *shitachi*. Shuffle the left foot forward a step followed by a step with the right foot and cut to the left side of shitachi's head. Maintain control over the centerline of the attack.

Shitachi: Step forward with the left foot then right foot, alternating until within cutting distance of *uchitachi*. As uchitachi attacks, shuffle the right foot back a step followed by a full step back with the left foot and perform a downward cut to block uchitachi's sword.

Note to Uchitachi and Shitachi: All cuts should be performed from a *jodan* position. Both combatants transition through jodan as their feet pass each other while stepping in *ayumi-ashi*.

3: **Uchitachi:** Shuffle forward with your right foot to pressure shitachi to move back. Step forward quickly with the left foot while performing a downward cut to the right side of shitachi's head. Maintain control of the centerline with the kissaki at the end of the cut.

Shitachi: Shuffle back with the left foot as uchitachi pressures your centerline. Step back with your right foot and cut downward from left to right to block uchitachi's cut to your head.

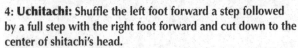

4: **Uchitachi:** Shuffle the left foot forward a step followed by a full step with the right foot forward and cut down to the center of shitachi's head.

Shitachi: Step back only with your left foot and perform a two-hand block directly overhead. The *tsuka* should be to your right and the *kissaki* to the left above the head. Receive the cut just in front of the head with both arms bent.

Note to Uchitachi and Shitachi: The end position of this cut leaves uchitachi's arms fully extended with very little power or mobility while shitachi's sword is ready to move just off of the centerline.

CONTINUED ON NEXT PAGE

5: Uchitachi: After the energy of your cut has been absorbed by shitachi's block, shuffle backward with the left foot while shitachi performs a *suriuke* block. Release the tsuka with your left hand as your sword's kissaki is thrown diagonally to your left rear corner. As you move back, lower your elbows downward while you try to regain control of the combative space.

Shitachi: From under the sword, perform a suriuke technique while you move forward and take uchitachi's balance. Use the momentum to throw uchitachi's sword to your right front corner while you attempt to regain control of the center line with your kissaki.

6: Uchitachi: Shuffle back with both feet as shitachi thrusts toward your right rib cage.

Shitachi: Try to find the opening *(suki)* in uchitachi's position while maintaining a position of defense that does not reveal your intentions. When you are satisfied that the centerline is open, immediately step forward with the left foot and perform a supported hand thrust *(soete tsuki)* to uchitachi's right rib cage. Continue to pressure uchitachi as he moves back to escape the thrust.

7: **Uchitachi:** Lower the sword to knee level and shuffle back a step with the left foot followed by the right foot. While shitachi regains a position on line in chudan no kamae, raise the sword to chudan no kamae. The swords should cross on the left side of each blade.

Shitachi: As uchitachi lowers the sword to *gedan* and then shuffles back, exert pressure on his centerline with the kissaki as you step forward with the right foot in chudan no kamae. Maintain pressure when uchitachi raises his sword to chudan no kamae.

8: **Uchitachi:** Turn the cutting edge of the sword inward toward shitachi's blade. Lower the sword simultaneously with shitachi into *gedan no kamae* while maintaining a connection to his sword along the cutting edge. Shuffle back a step with your left and then right foot. Release the connection to shitachi's sword at the kissaki as you both separate. Return to your original starting position by taking three or five steps back while maintaining gedan no kamae.

Shitachi: Turn the cutting edge of the sword inward toward uchitachi's blade. Lower the sword simultaneously with uchitachi into gedan no kamae while maintaining a connection to his sword along the cutting edge. Shuffle back a step with your left and then right foot. Release the connection to shitachi's sword at the kissaki as you both separate. Return to your starting original position by taking three or five steps back while maintaining gedan no kamae.

TSUBAMEGAESHI—TURNING SWALLOW

While you are walking, an opponent to your forward position attempts to cut you in a downward kiri-oroshi. You receive and stop his oncoming downward cut by retreating and performing a nukitsuke. Your counterattack stops his momentum and you both step into *hasso no kamae*. You seize the moment and move forward and attack with a right-to-left kiritsuke as you control the centerline. As the enemy retreats, you continue to pressure him and advance with a second kiritsuke to the opposite side. Your continued pressure forces the opponent back for the third time and you perform a downward kirioroshi. The opponent evades your third cut by stepping back into jodan no kamae. He then attacks with a downward kirioroshi to the center of your exposed head. His attack is nullified and then countered by either your choice of a flowing block *(ukenagashi)* followed by a kesa-giri cut to his neck or by a rising cut across his body that is followed by a horizontal cut to his neck. As the opponent submits and then retreats into chudan no kamae, you raise your sword and meet him in a chudan no kamae. The swordsmen then lower their swords to gedan no kamae. Both swordsmen return to the original starting positions.

TSUBAMEGAESHI—HOW TO DRAW THE SWORD

1: Uchitachi: Step forward with the right foot and draw the sword into *chudan no kamae*. Step forward with the left foot into *jodan no kamae*. Walk forward and close the distance to *shitachi* until you are within cutting range.

Shitachi: Stand confident in a natural posture while *uchitachi* closes within cutting distance.

2: Uchitachi: Shuffle the left foot forward a step followed by a step with the right foot forward and cut to the top of shitachi's head.

Shitachi: Step back with the left foot and perform a rising *nukitsuke* to block uchitachi's attack. Allow the sword to rise directly up the centerline as you step back and away from the attack. Put power in the *kissaki* and receive the attack with the power from your hips.

3: Uchitachi: Step back with the right foot to *hasso no kamae.*

Shitachi: Step back with the right foot to hasso no kamae.

4: Uchitachi: Shuffle back with the right foot as shitachi pressures your centerline. Step back with the left foot and cut downward from right to left to block shitachi's cut to your head.

Shitachi: Shuffle forward with your left foot to pressure uchitachi to move back. Step forward quickly with the right foot while performing a downward cut to the left side of uchitachi's head. Maintain control of the centerline with the kissaki at the end of the cut.

5: Uchitachi: Shuffle back with the left foot while shitachi pressures your centerline. Step back with the right foot and cut downward from left to right to block shitachi's cut to your head.

Shitachi: Shuffle forward with your right foot to pressure uchitachi to move back. Step forward quickly with the left foot while performing a downward cut to the right side of uchitachi's head. Maintain control of the centerline with the kissaki at the end of the cut.

CONTINUED ON NEXT PAGE

6: Uchitachi: Shuffle the right foot backward a step followed by a step with the left foot into jodan no kamae with both feet parallel to each other. Allow shitachi's sword to just miss your body as he cuts downward.

Shitachi: Shuffle forward with your left foot followed by a full step with your right foot. Step forward with the left foot until both feet are parallel to each other as you perform a downward *kirioroshi*. Allow your body to incline forward as you follow the sword through the cut.

Note to Uchitachi and Shitachi: The end position of this cut leaves shitachi's arms fully extended with the kissaki at uchitachi's knee level while shitachi's sword is ready to move just *off* of the centerline.

7: Uchitachi: Cut to shitachi's head with kirioroshi as you step forward with the right foot.

Shitachi: Shuffle the left foot off line a step to the left corner and perform a flowing block (*ukenagashi*). Allow the sword to rotate around clockwise through jodan no kamae and cut diagonally to uchitachi's neck.

KAE WAZA—VARIATION

Uchitachi: Cut to *shitachi's* head with *kirioroshi* as you step forward with the right foot.

Shitachi: Shuffle the left foot off line to the left corner a step and perform a diagonal upward cut across uchitachi's body. Pivot 90 degrees and perform a cut to uchitachi's neck.

8: **Uchitachi:** Lower the sword to knee level and shuffle back a step with the left foot followed by the right foot. As shitachi regains a position on line in chudan no kamae, raise the sword to chudan no kamae. The swords should cross on the left side of each blade.

Shitachi: As uchitachi lowers the sword to gedan and then shuffles back, exert pressure on his centerline with the kissaki. Step back on line with the right and then left foot. Maintain pressure as uchitachi raises his sword in to chudan no kamae.

9: **Uchitachi:** Turn the cutting edge of the sword inward toward shitachi's blade. Lower the sword simultaneously with shitachi into *gedan no kamae* while maintaining a connection to his sword along the cutting edge. Shuffle back a step with your left and then right foot. Release the connection to shitachi's sword at the kissaki as you both separate. Return to your original starting position by taking three or five steps back while maintaining gedan no kamae.

Shitachi: Turn the cutting edge of the sword inward toward uchitachi's blade. Lower the sword simultaneously with uchitachi into gedan no kamae while maintaining a connection to his sword along the cutting edge. Shuffle back a step with your left and then right foot. Release the connection to shitachi's sword at the kissaki as you both separate. Return to your original starting position by taking three or five steps back while maintaining gedan no kamae.

CHAPTER 9

SUEMONOGIRI—HISTORY AND PURPOSE OF TEST CUTTING

*T*ameshigiri or suemonogiri is a popular and enjoyable component of the practice and study of traditional Japanese sword arts. However, its place in the history of the Japanese sword arts and its relevance to the study of battojutsu is frequently misunderstood or overlooked. The most commonly understood definition of tameshigiri is "test-cutting," and it implies a testing of the blade. Within the older orthodox schools of Japanese sword arts, the term of suemonogiri was preferred, implying a testing of the swordsman's skill in cutting. According to Miura Takeyuki, the 20th soshihan of the Masaoka branch of Muso jikiden eishin-ryu, suemonogiri is also more ceremonial in nature.

Historically, one application of tameshigiri was the testing of *shinsaku-to* (newly forged blades), which were typically conducted by *tosho* (sword smiths) using straw or bamboo targets. Because it can imply the killing of another human being, tameshigiri was conducted before the final polish of the sword. When satisfied with the cutting capabilities of the blade, the tosho would purify the sword through prayer and ritual in order to remove any harmful spiritual energy that may have manifested in the sword as a result of the tameshigiri. The smith would thereby breath new spirit or life into the blade. After the final polish, the sword was presented to the samurai as pure and shining—free of harmful energy and impurities both spiritual and physical.

Originally tameshigiri may have been applied in executions or in acts of sacrifice to mythological gods, particularly in variations of blade testing used in other cultures. In feudal Japan, another historical application of tameshigiri involved the use of human corpses for testing the blades of many samurai. This practice became so common that at one point there was great demand for corpses for this purpose. Over time, however, the use of corpses for tameshigiri came to be viewed by many as barbaric. As a result, it became somewhat restricted, and in the Edo period, it was most often conducted in association with the punishment of convicted criminals. Test cutting for such purposes was most typically carried out by experts in the techniques of cutting, known as *tameshi-geisha* and *suemono-shi*. These men were typically lower-ranking members of the samurai class who were very skilled in kenjutsu.

Because of the historical applications of tameshigiri and the potentially harmful or negative spiritual energy that can be associated with it, negative connotations concerning tameshigiri have carried over into recent history. As recently as a half-century ago, tameshigiri was not usually conducted during *embu*. The places in which embu are conducted are frequently holy or special places. It was felt that the negative images and feelings tameshigiri brought, those of cutting human corpses, had the potential to contaminate the spiritual nature of embu and their associated locations. Certainly, no one would want to demonstrate the methods of their *ryu-ha* following a demonstration of tameshigiri.

Today, tameshigiri is viewed differently. It is a common element of demonstrations and has become a mode of competition in recent decades. In many ways, this is a positive evolution and can be an outlet for additional enjoyment of your practice. However, tameshigiri conducted for such purposes should be kept in proper perspective. While it may have many positive aspects, such as the development of focus, awareness, and sportsmanship, tameshigiri for such purposes is frequently conducted for the entertainment of spectators. Because of its intent, such tameshigiri may be viewed as *yugei* (performing art) rather than *bugei* (martial arts).

While the practice of tameshigiri is a valuable component of your training, understand that real skill in proper cutting is a direct result of the constant effort of the correct practice of waza and kumitachi of Eishin-ryu. This is most important. From a swordsman's perspective, proper cutting is really a product of the embodiment of the principles contained in the curriculum of the ryu. The attitude required for tameshigiri is very different in your individual practice when compared to embu; it is a personal study. Because of this reality of training, tameshigiri should be understood as *ura waza* (hidden techniques) of Eishin-ryu batto-ho. The authors' instruction in tameshigiri that was received from soshihan Miura illustrates this point well. The lesson consisted of one cut—that was it! And it was over in a less than a second. When he finished the cut, Miura discussed the importance of *kokyu*—of the hips and total body—and the connection to the target. This lesson imparted the knowledge that the swordsman and the target should be one and not two. He would finish his instruction by saying, "Have you got it? Now research and train yourself!"

Tameshigiri can be a useful part of practice and can help in your progress. In many ways, it is inseparable from kenjutsu and battojutsu. It can also be fun. However, it should be remembered that the practice of tameshigiri as part of your training in battojutsu is a personal study and should be approached with correct attitude and intent. Tameshigiri is a part of the total way to view technique; there is no need for fancy or showy cutting. Rather, it must be conducted with the same sincerity that you would practice waza or kumitachi. It must be practiced as budo.

DEVELOP THE SPIRIT OF KENKYU

Sometimes when you observe tameshigiri, you see a practitioner simply cutting mats rather than showing a demonstration of good technique derived from waza applied to tameshigiri. Tameshigiri such as this is *kyokugei* (for show), and while it may be a demonstration of successful cutting, it does not necessarily represent good technique. The purpose of tameshigiri in battojutsu is very different than performing tameshigiri for demonstrations. The correct incorporation of tameshigiri into batto practice requires *kenkyushin*. The word kenkyu means "research" or "advanced study." *Shin,* of course, refers to the mind. Therefore, kenkyushin means a deeply studying mind. For the practitioner of Eishin-ryu batto-ho, the main goal of *batto tameshigiri* is to cut using principles and techniques from the waza and kumitachi of the curriculum of the ryu. This is done through kenkyushin, which involves the advanced study of the toho (sword method) contained within the *waza* and kumitachi.

In basic tameshigiri, practitioners typically talk about cutting with the monouchi of the blade. However, battojutsu waza and kumitachi teach that, in addition to the monouchi, other cutting aspects of the blade are used in combat. For example, in the nukitsuke in junto sono ichi, the kissaki may be used to cut to the opponent's eyes. How is this understanding of the technique applied to tameshigiri? A correct nukitsuke using the kissaki cannot cut very deeply—perhaps only a few inches. If you attempt tameshigiri in order to practice cutting using this nukitsuke, even if you cut through the mat completely, the distance and therefore the technique itself was incorrect from the standpoint of the waza. The correct execution of tameshigiri using the waza as it is intended would be to cut one to three inches into the mat then to follow with kirioroshi using kesa-giri. (Remember that kesa-giri can be a form of kirioroshi.) In order to understand these techniques, the practitioner has to be able to cut the mat using them just as they are taught in the waza, then he can execute the finishing techniques. *Shato* is a good example of a waza using the middle of the blade—because of the maai—to execute batto tameshigiri. However, this time it is for the kirioroshi. The kumitachi of Eishin-ryu batto-ho also represent good sources of tameshigiri because you have to deal with the challenge of dynamic movement as practiced in the paired forms. It can be very difficult to cut correctly when moving because the body movement has to be correct in order to cut successfully. This practice is an effective way to train the eyes to acquire the target and identify the correct distancing while in motion.

One last but very important point in applying waza and kumitachi to batto tameshigiri is the understanding of how deeply the blade cuts or where the blade stops after a cut. A swordsman should develop precise control while still being able to cut. A method to practice this skill using tameshigiri involves rolling two or more mats, one rolled over another. Then, instead of cutting completely through the mats, try cutting through just one, leaving the other untouched. Or, cut through two mats out of three mats rolled together. You will find that it is much more difficult to cut through one mat and stop before cutting into second mat rather than just cutting right through both mats.

As is evidenced here, the waza and kumitachi of battojutsu, through the use of kenkyushin, are excellent sources to develop real cutting technique with control and precision. A practitioner has to understand the *bunkai* and toho of the waza, understanding that different parts of the blade can be used to cut in different ways. As an aside, this advanced approach to cutting multiple targets in tandem or using shortened cuts to simulate cutting with the kissaki should not be taught until a student is past the *kyusha* level and has reached the *yudansha* grades. Instead, kyusha should spend time becoming comfortable with the action, mechanics and distancing required for cutting a target by using the basic cutting patterns introduced later in this chapter. It should be clear that batto tameshigiri is very different from simply cutting mats. Mindless cutting has no benefit and in fact is merely a source of more trash being sent to a landfill and also a needless waste of money. Batto tameshigiri has real value and real benefits and is a practice to develop a deeper understanding of your overall sword training.

ALIGNMENT FOR TEST CUTTING

Distance and geometry are the key factors that must be understood to successfully perform test cutting. Each individual has a unique physique, range of motion and experience level. The differences in structures of the human body will not affect the geometry of cutting if the basic principles of correct alignment and distance are observed. Japanese katana are designed to cut as the blade moves in an arc. This geometric configuration of the sword allows the blade to make contact with the target at a single point along the cutting edge as it passes through the target material. The geometry of the blade is such that any misalignment of the body to the target during the swing of the sword will result in a failed cut.

As the sword is swung toward the target, it moves in a forward arc away from the practitioner until it crosses the furthest point of reach from the body. This forward point is the critical point of contact. As the monouchi (striking point) of the sword passes this point, it begins to travel back toward the practitioner. Because of the geometry of the blade, the contact point on the sword continues to pass through the target in succession as this point on the blade continues to move past the practitioner's centerline of full extension.

Proper body alignment to the target material increases the effectiveness of the cut and maximizes the efficient transfer of power from the axis of the cutting arc to the contact point on the sword. This body alignment should be practiced on stationary targets for a prolonged period before attempting to cut a moving target. Each series of alignments and cutting angles presents its own unique characteristics because of differences in how a person grips the tsuka to facilitate the cut. Any excessive body movement that alters the natural arc of the swing will negate its cutting power.

> **CAUTION:** Special attention should be given to correct leg position during each of the cutting series presented in this book. All downward cuts should be executed in the direction of the rear leg. Incorrect leg position will lead to serious injury during a failed or over exaggerated cut. Should the blade wander or be misdirected as it leaves the target material, the sword will travel upward or downward in a severe arc that will endanger your forward leg or foot.

LEG POSITIONING

1: This is the correct leg position for cutting a right-to-left *kesa-giri*.

2: This is the incorrect leg position for a right-to-left kesa-giri.

ALIGNMENT FOR A LEFT-TO-RIGHT ANGULAR DOWNWARD CUT—KESA-GIRI

1: Prepare by standing directly in front of the target in *jodan no kamae.* The target should bisect the body vertically in this position. The cutting edge of the blade should face upward with the *kissaki* facing directly to the rear at a 45-degree angle.

2: Create a 45-degree angle with the sword by rotating the wrists counterclockwise to the left. Maintain the same vertical and horizontal planes as you create the angle of the cut. Refrain from allowing the kissaki to move clockwise or counterclockwise around your head.

3: Step forward with the left leg and align the right shoulder with the center of the target. The sword will intersect the left edge of the target as it passes the centerline of the swordsman's body during the cut.

ALIGNMENT FOR A RIGHT-TO-LEFT ANGULAR DOWNWARD CUT—KESA-GIRI

1: Prepare by standing directly in front of the target in *jodan no kamae.* The target should bisect the body vertically in this position. The cutting edge of the blade should face upward with the *kissaki* facing directly to the rear at a 45-degree angle.

2: Create a 45-degree angle with the sword by rotating the wrists clockwise to the right. Maintain the same vertical and horizontal planes as you create the angle of the cut. Refrain from allowing the kissaki to move clockwise or counterclockwise around your head.

3: Step forward with the right leg and align the left shoulder with the center of the target. The sword will intersect the right edge of the target as it passes the centerline of the swordsman's body during the cut.

ALIGNMENT FOR A LEFT AND RIGHT RISING CUT—KIRIAGE

1: Left Kiriage Position: Prepare by standing to the left side of the target in *hidari waki no kamae*. The target should bisect the body vertically through the right shoulder in this position. The cutting edge of the blade should face downward with the *kissaki* facing directly to the rear at a 45-degree angle.

2: Right Kiriage Position: Prepare by standing to the right side of the target in *migi waki no kamae*. The target should bisect the body vertically through the left shoulder in this position. The cutting edge of the blade should face downward with the kissaki facing directly to the rear at a 45 degree angle.

ALIGNMENT FOR A LEFT AND RIGHT HORIZONTAL CUT—SUIHEI

1: Right Suihei Position: Prepare by standing to the right side of the target in *migi waki no kamae*. Practice this position with the feet parallel to each other with the body weight distributed evenly over both feet. The target should bisect the body vertically through the centerline of the body in front of the left shoulder. The cutting edge of the blade should be in the horizontal position and parallel to the ground on the right side of the body. The *kissaki* projects to the right.

2: Left Suihei Position: Prepare by standing to the left side of the target in *hidari waki no kamae*. Practice this position with your feet parallel to each other with the body weight distributed evenly over both feet. The target should bisect the body vertically through the centerline of the body in front of the right shoulder. The cutting edge of the blade should be in the horizontal position and parallel to the ground on the left side of the body. The kissaki projects to the left.

KIRI-MA—CUTTING DISTANCE

To create the correct kiri-ma between the swordsman and the target, it is imperative to first develop a consistent sword swing. When the length of the cutting stroke remains constant, the study of cutting distance becomes a study of the body's proximity to the target. Beginners often find that their ability to cut the target at various heights is challenged because of inconsistency in the size, arc and power of their cutting stroke. The geometry of the blade is such that it will slice more efficiently as the edge is moved across the target in a wider arc.

For cutting, correct technique is far more important than muscular strength. Full extension of the sword creates greater centripetal force. Therefore, a larger cutting arc creates greater velocity at the monouchi and kissaki. The bigger the cutting stroke, the easier it is to cut. It is also important to note that a wider arc allows the sword to cut through targets of greater diameter and density. Centripetal force is the key to a cut that will sever multiple targets in a single stroke. The path to developing this kind of force lies in learning to cut from the hips in order to create a larger arc and greater speed.

Proper repeated practice of kihon techniques and waza will establish and reinforce the correct combination of te no uchi (grip), hasuji otosu (straight alignment of the cutting edge), and enshin-ryoku (centripetal force). These fundamentals of a correct cutting stroke must be applied during the practice of waza. The consistency of the cutting form must correspond to correct kamae (attitude and posture), kuzushi (balance) and iaigoshi (hip connection). Regulating the consistency and speed of the basic swing will facilitate an easy transition between waza, kumitachi and tameshigiri.

Once you have developed a correct swing, tameshigiri becomes a matter of correctly applying that swing to the target. When the kamae, swing, and iaigoshi are consistent, it becomes easier to establish the correct kiri-ma. The monouchi should intersect the target approximately 10 inches back from the kissaki. Even though sword lengths vary depending on the swordsman's preferences, it will usually require at least this much monouchi to cut through two rolled *wara* (rolled bamboo-mat targets). It is better to establish a larger swing and therefore a bigger arc during the early stage of practice even though smaller diameter targets are being cut.

Note that the natural full extension of the sword at shoulder height should bring the monouchi into contact with the target at the correct position to take advantage of the maximum speed that is established during the swing. For basic cutting, the shoulders are the pivotal axis for the arc of the swing. When the monouchi crosses the vertical plane of the shoulders, it releases its energy and begins to travel back toward the swordsman. During the continuation of the swing, the cutting energy is delivered incrementally outward from the monouchi to the tip of the kissaki as the contact point of the sword passes through the greatest extension of the arc from the shoulders. Establish the habit of adjusting the body's relative position to the target in order to correct any distance issues. Do not change the size or extension of the stroke to correct the kiri-ma.

CUTTING DISTANCE

1: The correct distance for the first cut on the top of a target places the back end of the *monouchi* fully on the *wara* at shoulder height.

2: This is the incorrect distance at shoulder height.

As the targeted area of the *wara* drops below the level of the practitioner's shoulders at full extension, it becomes necessary to reestablish the cutting distance. A lower target area increases the distance to the target. Most beginners find it easy to complete a first cut at shoulder height and then fail to correct the relative distance from the shoulders to the targeted area of the wara.

CORRECTING CUTTING DISTANCE

1: Incorrect distance does not allow for enough *monouchi* to cut through the target. Incorrect *kiri-ma* should be corrected by moving the entire body forward or by lowering the hips in a deeper *iaigoshi*. These two options bring the shoulders in closer proximity to the targeted area and allow the *monouchi* to make contact at the proper point. Do not lean forward with the upper body or rotate the shoulders to reestablish the cutting distance. Good balance and correct *shisei* (posture) must be maintained at all times.

2: Shuffle the right leg forward a step or lower the hips and shoulders to reestablish the correct distance.

There is no need for fear or anxiety as the length of the wara decreases. If the target is as wide as the sword, the target is not more difficult to cut. Sword placement is the only issue of concern to those who are new to tameshigiri. However as you continue to practice good cutting habits and proper distancing, the correct blade placement on the target will become second nature.

CUTTING SMALLER TARGETS

1-4: Do not allow your confidence to be cut down as the length of the *wara* decreases in size. As the target becomes smaller in size, it becomes a psychological barrier for many new swordsmen. To maintain your confidence, place rubber bands or some other soft fastening material around the wara to establish specific target areas. Cutting to these points takes the mystery out of cutting a wara that seems to get smaller. The more accurate the strokes become, the less you will experience anxiety as the target appears to shrink in size.

PREPARATION FOR TEST CUTTING

The target material of choice for tameshigiri cutting practice is the *tatami omote*. They are the outside wrapping of rice straw mats that cover the floors of a traditional Japanese home. Each mat is approximately six feet long by three feet wide. All traditional Japanese rooms are built to accommodate an exact number of these mats.

The interior section of the *tatami* is a layered stuffing of straw material that is bound together and then covered by the more esthetically pleasing tatami omote (face) covering. The edges are protected by borders of fabric that bind it all together. The top cover of the tatami becomes worn over time and needs to be replaced by fresh, clean coverings. In the past, it was the discarded tatami omote that were acquired by swordsman for testing their cutting ability. Unfortunately, these used tatami omote retain the dirt and grit from years of exposure to the elements. They will scratch or damage a sword as the blade passes through the target. Used tatami are like a box of chocolates in that you never truly know what you are going to get. They do not offer consistent feedback to the swordsman, and if used for competition cutting, they create an uneven playing field because of their inconsistency.

Manufacturers and distributors now export new tatami omote for the sole purpose of supplying cutting materials for enthusiasts of Japanese sword arts. It is advisable to obtain new tatami for test cutting whenever possible. These new covers offer a smooth even surface and bear a distinct aroma of freshly cut straw. The proper way to roll these mats is along their edges to form a three-foot long target. Each rolled mat should then be secured with heavy rubber bands or tied with rice straw hemp to ensure their stability and form. These rolled mats are called *wara*. When submerged and soaked under water for up to 24 hours the tatami omote or wara develop the density and feel of a body when being cut. The water also lubricates the blade as it passes through the target. New tatami are of a consistent density and this makes them uniformly better for judging your cutting ability.

The most important admonition for every student to master is "safety first in all pursuits." It is imperative to inspect all parts of the sword and saya for defects and flaws. It needs to be said that all swords are not created equally. But for cutting practice, they should all be within a certain range of sharpness to allow for a fair evaluation of your cutting ability. As a standard rule, if a sword will not cut through a single sheet of paper held at arm's reach with one hand, it will not cut tatami omote properly either. Even the best technique by a master practitioner is diminished by a dull sword. If a sword is dull or bent, it should be immediately retired until it has been repaired by a professional.

Proper etiquette should also be observed each time the waza of the cutting patterns are performed. Each of the accompanying series of instructions must be preceded with the reiho when practiced. Consider the saho and the reiho as part of the tameshigiri waza. As a part of the etiquette, always perform a check of the *mekugi* as well as examining the overall fitness of the sword. These practices ensure the proper attitude and contribute to the overall safety that is necessary when handling a sharp sword. Before cutting, perform hai-rei and to-rei. Then perform a *moku-rei* in the direction of the target that is to be cut. These steps must be taken each time training begins.

CUTTING PATTERNS FOR EISHIN-RYU BATTO-HO TAMESHIGIRI

The collection of patterns listed here were assembled to teach the practitioner various responses to battlefield situations. Each individual pattern should be researched deeply to understand the subtle characteristic in timing and distance required for each set. The timing of the cuts should be grouped in pairs so as to facilitate a change in timing during the reversal of the sword's cutting direction. Even though the cutting directions may seem similar, each set is unique in that the timing changes the degree of difficulty as the number of cuts increase in each set. These patterns should be practiced by mirror image in addition to how they are illustrated here.

SIX SUEMONOGIRI EXERCISES

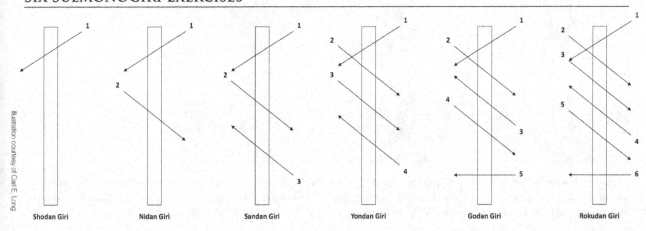

Shodan Giri   Nidan Giri   Sandan Giri   Yondan Giri   Godan Giri   Rokudan Giri

SHODAN GIRI—CUT ONE DIRECTION AND LEVEL

1: Step forward and grasp the *saya* with the left hand.

2: Perform a standing bow.

3: Withdraw the sword from the *saya* and perform a routine check of the *mekugi* and other *koshirae*.

4: Step forward with the right leg and assume *chudan no kamae*.

5: Step forward with the left foot into *jodan no kamae* and directly in line with the target.

6: Step forward with the left foot to position and perform a left-to-right *kesa-giri*.

7: Step back with the left foot and in line with the target and assume jodan no kamae.

8: Continue to repeat steps five through seven until you feel comfortable cutting left to right. Change feet and take a stance with the right foot forward. Change the direction of the downward *kesa-giri* and practice cutting from right to left with the right foot forward.

9: Perform yoko chiburi, *shoden noto* **and then return to the starting position.**

10: Finish the *waza* **by performing a standing bow.**

Note: This is a basic exercise and should be practiced until the angle of the cut is consistently performed at 45 degrees. Do not attempt any further exercises until both right and left kesa-giri is consistently adequate.

NIDAN GIRI—CUT TWO DIRECTIONS AND LEVELS

1: Step forward and grasp the *saya* with the left hand.

2: Perform a standing bow.

3: Withdraw the sword from the *saya* and perform a routine check of the *mekugi* and other *koshirae*.

4: Step forward with the right leg and assume *chudan no kamae*.

5: Step forward with the left foot into *jodan no kamae* and directly in line with the target.

6: Step forward with the left foot to perform a left-to-right *kesa-giri*.

7: Step back with the left foot and place the body in line with the target while assuming jodan no kamae.

8: Step forward with the right foot closer to the target for a lower cut.

9: Perform a right-to-left kesa-giri.

10: Step back with the left foot followed by the right foot and then left foot into chudan no kamae.

11: Perform *yoko chiburi*.

12: Perform *shoden noto*.

13: Step back to the starting position.

14: Perform a standing bow.

SANDAN GIRI—CUT THREE DIRECTIONS AND LEVELS

1: Step forward and grasp the *saya* with the left hand.

2: Perform a standing bow.

3: Withdraw the sword from the saya and perform a routine check of the *mekugi* and other *koshirae*.

4: Step forward with the right leg and assume *chudan no kamae*.

5: Step forward with the left foot into *jodan no kamae* and directly in line with the target.

6: Step forward with the left foot and perform a left-to-right *kesa-giri*.

7: Step back with the left foot and place the body in line with the target while assuming jodan no kamae.

8: Step forward with the right foot closer to the target for a lower cut.

9: Perform a right-to-left kesa-giri.

10: Lower the sword to a low *hidari waki no kamae* position with the cutting edge facing forward and down.

11: Perform a left-to-right *kiriage*.

12: Step back with the right foot and then left foot through jodan no kame and into chudan no kamae.

13: Perform *yoko chiburi, shoden noto* and then return to the starting position.

14: Finish the *waza* by performing a standing bow.

217

YONDAN GIRI—CUT FOUR DIRECTIONS AND LEVELS

1: Step forward and grasp the *saya* with the left hand.

2: Perform a standing bow.

3: Withdraw the sword from the saya and perform a routine check of the *mekugi* and other *koshirae*.

4: Step forward with the right leg and assume *chudan no kamae.*

5: Step forward with the left foot into *jodan no kamae* and directly in line with the target.

6: Step forward with the left foot and perform a left-to-right *kesa-giri.*

7: Step back with the left foot and place the body in line with the target while assuming jodan no kamae.

8: Step forward with the right foot closer to the target for a lower cut.

9: Perform a right-to-left kesa-giri.

10: Raise the sword in jodan no kamae and adjust the cutting distance to the target.

11: Perform another right-to-left kesa-giri.

12: Reverse the sword direction for an up-ward cut.

13: Perform a left-to-right *kiriage*.

14: Step back with the right foot then left through jodan no kamae into chudan no kamae.

15: Perform *yoko chiburi, shoden noto* and then return to the starting position.

16: Finish the *waza* by performing a standing bow.

GODAN GIRI—CUT FIVE DIRECTIONS AND LEVELS

1: Step forward and grasp the *saya* with the left hand.

2: Perform a standing bow.

3: Withdraw the sword from the saya and perform a routine check of the *mekugi* and other *koshirae*.

4: Step forward with the right leg and assume *chudan no kamae.*

5: Step forward with the left foot into *jodan no kamae* and directly in line with the target.

6: Step forward with the left foot and perform a left-to-right *kesa-giri*.

7: Step back with the left foot and place the body in line with the target while assuming jodan no kamae.

8: Step forward with the right foot to move the body closer to the target for a lower cut.

9: Perform a right-to-left kesa-giri.

10: Lower the sword to a low *hidari waki no kamae* position with the cutting edge facing forward and down.

11: Perform a left-to-right kiriage.

12: Assume jodan no kamae and reverse the cutting direction of the sword.

13: Perform a right-to-left kesa-giri.

14: Step the left foot forward so that the feet are parallel to each other and to the target. Position the sword to the left side of the body on a horizontal plane.

15: Perform a horizontal cut from left to right by turning the hips.

16: Step back with the right foot and then left foot through jodan no kamae into chudan no kamae.

7: Perform *yoko chiburi, shoden noto* and then return to the starting position.

CONTINUED ON NEXT PAGE

18: Finish the *waza* by performing a standing bow.

ROKUDAN GIRI—CUT SIX DIRECTIONS AND LEVELS

1: Step forward and grasp the *saya* with the left hand.

2: Perform a standing bow.

3: Withdraw the sword from the saya and perform a routine check of the *mekugi* and other *koshirae*.

4: Step forward with the right leg and assume *chudan no kamae*.

5: Step forward with the left foot into *jodan no kamae* and directly in line with the target.

6: Step forward with the left foot and perform a left-to-right *kesa-giri*.

7: Step back with the left foot and place the body in line with the target while assuming jodan no kamae.

8: Step forward with the right foot to move the body closer to the target for a lower cut.

9: Perform a right-to-left kesa-giri.

10: Raise the sword to jodan no kamae.

11: Perform a right-to-left kesa-giri.

12: Lower the sword to a low *hidari waki no kamae* position with the cutting edge facing forward and down.

13: Perform a left-to-right *kiriage*.

14: Assume jodan no kamae and reverse the cutting direction of the sword.

15: Perform a right-to-left kesa-giri.

16: Step the left foot forward so that the feet are parallel to each other and to the target. Position the sword to the left side of the body on a horizontal plane.

17: Perform a horizontal cut from left to right by turning the hips.

CONTINUED ON NEXT PAGE

18: Step back with the right foot and then left foot through jodan no kamae into chudan no kamae.

19: Perform *yoko chiburi, shoden noto* and then return to the starting position.

20: Finish the *waza* by performing a standing bow.

APPENDIX A
SWORD NOMENCLATURE AND CARE

Japanese terminology is used throughout this book as it is in many traditional dojo around the world. The Japanese language is the universally recognized language of *budo*. In particular, the nomenclature of the *katana*, the Japanese sword, must be memorized if you expect to study under the guidance of a traditional sword instructor.

The fully assembled sword is referred to as the katana. Katana is the general term used for Japanese swords within a particular range of length. More specifically, it is called a *daito* (long sword). This term is used to distinguish it from the *shoto* (short sword). The shoto or *wakizashi* was the companion sword worn in conjunction with the daito. Together they were the symbol of the samurai warrior class. The terminology is very specific to the katana and wakizashi. The *koshirae* (furniture) is all of the parts that are mounted on the *toshin* (bare blade). Each individual part plays an integral role in the performance of the sword. It is necessary to understand their functions in order to perform routine inspection and maintenance should the need arise.

The unsharpened sword used for *battojutsu* training is referred to as an *iaito* (practice sword). The sword used for *suemonogiri* (test cutting) is a sharpened blade called a *shinken* (spirit sword). The term shinken denotes the fact that it is a "live sword." Whether an iaito or a shinken is being used for practice, constant respect and attention should be given to the lethality of the sword.

KATANA NO MEISHO—PARTS OF THE SWORD

These are the parts of the katana that are most frequently discussed throughout the instructional chapters in the book. A working knowledge of all of the parts listed in the illustration on page 226 is highly recommended. The most important parts of the sword for the beginning student to remember are:

Japanese Term	Pronunciation	English Term
tsuka	ts'oo-kah	handle
tsuka gashira	ts'soo-kah-gah-shee-rah	end of handle
mekugi	meh-koo-gee	retaining peg
tsuba	ts'oo-bah	guard
saya	sah-yah	scabbard
koiguchi	coy-goo-ch'ee	mouth of the scabbard
kojiri	ko-e-jee-ree	butt of the scabbard
sageo	sah-gay-oh	scabbard strings
monouchi	moe-no-oo-chee	cutting section of the blade
ha or shiraha	haw (she-rah-haw)	sharp side of the blade
mune or mine	(moo-neh) mee-neh	spine or back of the blade
kissaki	kees-sak-kee	point of the blade
shinogi	shee-no-gee	upperside of the blade

PARTS OF THE KATANA

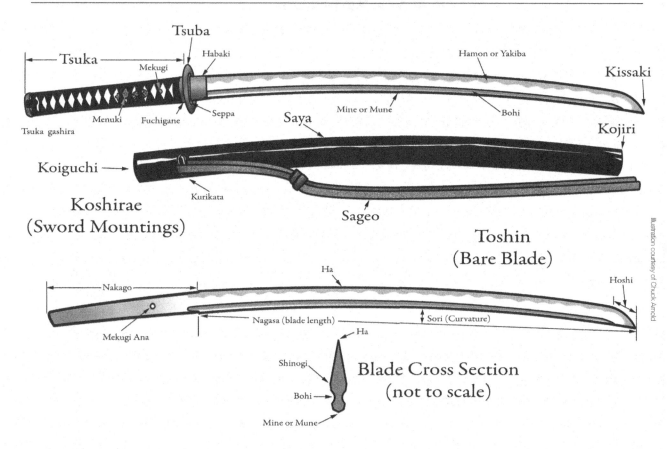

Tsuba

Tsuka   Habaki   Hamon or Yakiba   Kissaki

Mekugi

Menuki   Fuchigane   Seppa   Mine or Mune   Bohi

Tsuka gashira   Saya   Kojiri

Koiguchi

Kurikata

**Koshirae
(Sword Mountings)**   Sageo

**Toshin
(Bare Blade)**

Illustration courtesy of Chuck Arnold

Ha   Hoshi

Nakago

Nagasa (blade length)   Sori (Curvature)

Mekugi Ana   Ha

Shinogi

Bohi   **Blade Cross Section
(not to scale)**

Mine or Mune

SWORD MAINTENANCE

There is always maintenance required for authentic training weapons. Daily inspection for imperfections and damage is imperative. Occasionally, it may be necessary to oil or sand imperfections or dings found in wooden weapons. If they are found to be splintered or cracked, it is recommended they be retired immediately. Iaito, which are aluminum alloy and stainless steel swords, require thoughtful care and attention to the blade, scabbard and furniture surrounding the blade. These can become worn or damaged and should be repaired immediately on discovering such issues. Real swords (shinken) demand the most attention. Chips or cracks in any part of the sword or its furniture should be given special consideration before continued use. Steel corrodes on contact with moisture and oxygen. Therefore changes in temperature and humidity affect both the blade and the koshirae. Daily inspection and cleaning is necessary to maintain the quality and consistency of a superior performing sword.

Following each training session, the blade needs to be wiped clean of all moisture and residue that has accumulated. A complete disassembly of the blade is not necessary every time. However, the following steps should be taken on a regular basis for shinken made of carbon steel. There are times when you will only need to do a quick cleaning by wiping away the excess oil, followed by cleaning and re-oiling the blade and then replacing it in the saya. A full cleaning is not always necessary but must be done on a regular basis, particularly when the climate is humid or usage is more pronounced. If you desire your sword to have a long productive lifespan, attention to its proper care is essential.

First you'll need a proper cleaning kit that consists of high quality paper *(nuguikami)*, whetstone powder *(uchiko)*, a sword hammer and peg remover *(mekugi-nuki)*, rust-preventative mineral oil *(choji* oil) and soft paper or cloth for distributing the oil. These kits are easily purchased from major martial arts equipment suppliers. Higher quality uchiko and oil produce better cleaning results.

However, please remember that special care is required when performing the inspection and cleaning the shinken. Specific tools are necessary and should be acquired by all swordsmen. These tools are essential even for the regular basic maintenance of cleaning, straightening and sharpening training swords. It is not recommended to sharpen or attempt to straighten a bent blade until having received specialized training to do so. Improper attempts to straighten or sharpen a shinken can result in injury to yourself and permanent damage to the blade. It is also not recommended to perform any cleaning or servicing of the blade until you have received supervised guidance in the handling of a sharp sword.

SWORD MAINTENANCE EQUIPMENT

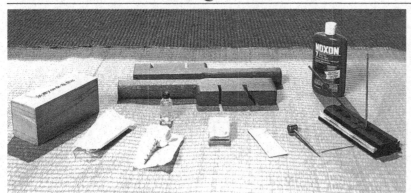

First Row (Left to Right): storage box, *nuguikami* (cleaning paper), *uchiko* (powder ball), *choji* oil, oil pad, *mekugi-nuki* (hammer), ceramic sharpener.

Second Row (Left to Right): sword-straightening sticks, metal polish.

EXAMINING THE SWORD

1: Begin by opening up the cleaning kit and preparing all of the materials. Pour a small amount of oil on the cloth. Have your cleaning paper and *uchiko* ball prepared, as well. Prior preparation of the tools allows for less action while holding a sharp blade and will lessen the chances of injury.

CONTINUED ON NEXT PAGE

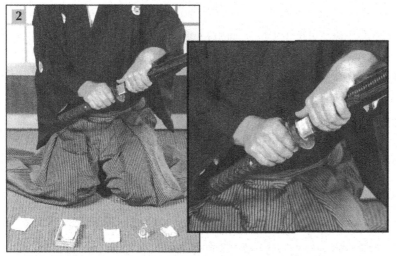

3: Once the *habaki* is free of the koi-guchi, support the sword with the right hand and reverse the left-hand grip on the saya. Grasp the saya with the left hand from the backside of the blade and begin to lift the saya off of the blade.

2: Bring the sword to the front and hold the *tsuka* in the right hand. Tilt the *saya* upward at an angle to the front with the cutting edge facing upward. Separate the sword from the saya by pushing forward on the *tsuba* with the left thumb.

4: Support the sword by placing the *tsuka gashira* on the right hip. Continue to pull the saya off of the blade.

5: Place the saya next to your right side with the *koiguchi* facing to the rear.

6: Hold the sword on the right hip with both hands. Examine the condition of the blade at the *kissaki*. Check for nicks or imperfections.

7: Scan the blade from the kissaki to the habaki looking for flaws or signs of unusual wear.

8: Turn the blade over and repeat the process of examination on the opposite side.

9: If you are satisfied that there are no serious flaws or conditions that require the services of a professional sword polisher, continue cleaning the blade.

CLEANING THE SWORD

1: With the *tsuka gashira* planted firmly against the right hip and braced by the right hand, turn the cutting edge upward. Reach down and pick up the small oiled cloth with the left hand. Starting near the *habaki*, fold the oiled cloth around the back unsharpened side of the sword. Hold the cloth so that both sides of the blade are lightly pinched between the fingers and thumb of the left hand. The *mune* should be resting on the middle of the small oiled cloth. Apply pressure to the side of the blade and wipe upward from the habaki to the *kissaki* in one direction. Place the oiled cloth back in the tray.

2: Choose a dry cloth or clean paper and wipe the oil and residue off of the blade starting at the habaki and moving toward the kissaki.

CONTINUED ON NEXT PAGE

3: Place the used paper to the side. Grasp the *tsuka* with the left hand and hold the tsuka gashira against the left hip. Pick up the *uchiko* with the right hand. Tap upward along both sides of the blade. On the final pass, apply the uchiko to the mune.

4: Replace the uchiko in the right hand with a clean piece of paper. Wrap the paper around the back of the sword. Cradle the mune between the fingers and thumb of the right hand near the habaki. Apply lateral pressure to the sides of the blade and wipe toward the kissaki. Fold the paper again to a clean side and repeat the wiping process from the habaki. Repeat this process until all debris and oil are removed.

5: Place the used paper to the side and reexamine both sides of the sword for any flaws or imperfections.

6: Pick up the oiled cloth and reapply a light coat of oil.

7: Reach down and back with the left hand and pick up the *saya* near the *koiguchi*.

8: Lift the koiguchi to the kissaki from underneath and begin to lower the saya onto the sword.

9: When the habaki enters the saya, push down lightly on the saya to secure the koiguchi to the habaki until it reaches the *tsuba*.

10: Raise the sword to forehead height with the tsuka pointed to the left. End by performing *to-rei* with the cutting edge facing the forehead.

APPENDIX B

THE EVOLUTION OF BATTOJUTSU

Today practitioners of *battojutsu*, also known as *iaijutsu*, practice the 450-year-old art of Japanese swordsmanship to develop their *kokoro* (minds and hearts) as well as their fighting skills. The emphasis has evolved and adapted throughout the history of Japanese fencing. The modern emphasis of battojutsu is better understood by examining its history and development over four-and-a-half centuries of evolution from its dark inception to its present-day form.

FIRST GENERATION:
HAYASHIZAKI JINSUKE MINAMOTO NO SHIGENOBU, (1546-1621)

Photo taken at Honbu dojo in Neyagawa-shi, Japan in 2000 by Carl E. Long.

流祖林崎甚助重信公御神像

Hayashizaki Jinsuke Shigenobu

Hayashizaki Jinsuke Shigenobu is supposed to have lived near the end of the Muramachi period. He is reported to have lived between the years 1546-1621, although the actual dates of his birth and death remain somewhat of a mystery. His place of birth was in northeastern Japan in Tateoka Oshu now known as Murayama City in Yamagata prefecture. At 14 years of age, Hayashizaki prepared to avenge the death of his father by another samurai and protect his family's honor. He made his way to Hayashizaki village. It is said that Hayashizaki secluded himself in the Tenshinsho Hayashizaki Myojin shrine for nearly 100 days and prayed to the spirit of Hayashi Myojin for divine inspiration. At the shrine, he received what he understood to be the inspiration for a new method of sword techniques that he referred to as *muso-ken* (dream sword). Records of the time indicate that the old man of the shrine imparted the inspiration for using a sword with a long hilt and drawing it from the scabbard in a fashion that allowed it to cut an opponent in a single action. Even though the techniques of drawing a sword and cutting had been practiced in other sword schools before Hayashizaki's enlightenment, he and his students are credited as having formulated the art on a greater scale than any of his predecessors. It is for this reason that he is considered the founder of the art of battojutsu.

Hayashizaki resided for many of his years in the town of Bushu. He was claimed to have been a devout believer in the Shinto religion, offering prayers and practicing austere Shinto rituals at the local shrine in Bushu. It is here that he cultivated his fighting style and taught members of his family his newly formed sword art, which he called *Hayashizaki shinmei muso-ryu*. His fighting style included the use of both a long sword that measured 39.37 inches as well as a shorter sword of 11.34 inches.

His reputation quickly spread, and Hayashizaki attracted many *kenjutsu* students who wished to advance their own skills and reputations. Many famous swordsmen adopted his methods and formed their own unique styles of combat. These students in turn continued to teach Hayashizaki shinmei muso-ryu as well as developed their own styles. In 1616, at approximately the age of 69 and having passed his sword methods on to a great many students, Hayashizaki set out on a four-year training pilgrimage. He never returned from this journey alive, and following his death, he was enshrined in the Hayashizaki Myojin shrine. This shrine is still located approximately one mile north of Tateoka station on the Hayashizaki Ou train line in the city of Murayama in Yamagata prefecture.

Among the many students of Hayashizaki were Katayama Hoki no Kami Fujiwara no Hisayasu, who was the founder of *Hoki-ryu;* Sekiguchi Hachiroemon Jushin, who was the founder of *Sekiguchi-ryu;* and Takamatsu Nobukatsu, who was the founder of *Ichinomiya-ryu.* Each of these men went on to propagate their own sword style based on the original teachings of Hayashizaki. But it is the authors' lineage from Hayashizaki that is followed in this book. This lineage was passed on by another of Hayashizaki's students: Tamiya Heibei Shigemasa.

Second Generation:
Tamiya Heibei Shigemasa (Narimasa), (d. 1670)

In the late 1500s, Tamiya was born in Iwamurata in Joshu or modern-day Gunma prefecture in the Kanto region of Japan. His full name was Tamiya Taira no Hyoe Shigemasa and he later changed it to Tsushima. He became a student of Hayashizaki after having studied Hazashizaki shinmei muso-ryu under Toshimotsuke no Kami Moriharu. But it was under the guidance of Hayashizaki that he mastered the true essence of the drawing-and-cutting *ryu* in a single action. Ancient records indicate that his swordsmanship reached divine levels and that he most likely was equal to the founder in his skills and ability. Tamiya founded the *Tamiya-ryu* style of battojutsu. His students would go on to establish a wide range of kenjutsu and battojutsu methods.

THIRD GENERATION:
NAGANO MURAKU NYŪDŌ KINROSAI, (B. LATE 1500S)

Nagano Muraku Kinrosai was the third inheritor in the line of teaching of Hayashizaki shinmei muso-ryu. He was also a direct disciple of Tamiya. Very little is known about his youth other than that in his childhood years he was known as Jurozaemon. Muraku's lineage descended from the family of Shinano no Kami, who was the samurai of Minowa castle in Joshu now Gumma prefecture. In the service of the Shinano family, Muraku rose to the rank of general. In 1542, the Shinano clan fell to the forces of Takeda Shingen in a war that had lasted for four years. Following the disbandment of the Shinano clan, Muraku traveled about perfecting his skills and seeking employment. Eventually he served as a samurai for Naomasa Ii, who was the lord of Hikone (Shiga prefecture). While serving Naomasa Ii, Muraku received wages of 500 *koku* of rice per year. It is rumored that Muraku may have traveled to the Northern provinces, and this is where he probably met Hayashizaki with whom he studied fencing. Although Muraku may have taken Hayashizaki as his teacher, it is more likely that he was extensively educated by Tamiya. It is also reported that Muraku died in Hikone at 90 years of age. Though his skills were great, Muraku did not delegate any single individual to pass on the teachings of Hayshizaki. Instead, as was the custom, Muraku passed along his knowledge to several of his students who then formed their own lines of transmission. Many of these schools continue to flourish today.

As such, Muraku is credited with several styles. There is his own family style of *Muraku-ryu* and the passing on of Hayashizaki's teachings. The student that passed on his Muraku-ryu was primarily Kamiizumi Magojiro Yoshitane. In the late, 20th century, the Muraku-ryu was led by Sasamori Junzo (1886-1976), who was a former member of the upper house of Japan's parliament. Among his many accomplishments like becoming the *soke* of several kenjutsu styles—Muraku-ryu, Hayashizaki shinmei muso-ryu, *Onno-ha itto-ryu* and *Chokugen-ryu naginatajutsu*—Sasamori Junzo was an avowed pacifist who devoted his life to giving the art of fencing educational and spiritual roles in a student's life. He passed the lineage of all four *koryu* to his son Sasamori Takemi. Momo Gunbei no Jo Mitsushige was the last direct student in the line of Muraku. Gunbei was also the student who continued Hayashizaki's sword school through another line of teaching.

FOURTH GENERATION:
MOMO GUNBEI NO JO MITSUSHIGE, (B. LATE 1500S)

Gunbei was the last student of Muraku to receive full transmission of his art. Little is known about his life other than that he passed the teachings of Hayashizaki on to a fifth generation of sword masters.

FIFTH GENERATION:
ARIKAWA SHOZAEMON MUNETSUGU, (B. LATE 1500S)

It is known that Arikawa Shozaemon Munetsugu served as a vassal of Toyotomi Hideyoshi (1536-1598), but otherwise, there is not much else known about him. The records of the ninth headmaster of Hayashizaki shinmei muso-ryu are the first indication of Arikawa's lineage to Hayashizaki's line in the historical record.

SIXTH GENERATION:
BANNO DANEMON NO JO NOBUSADA, (B. LATE 1500S)

Banno Danemon no Jo Nobusada taught Hayashizaki's sword-drawing method in Edo, which would become modern Tokyo. It was during this time in Japan that the most significant development in the history of battojutsu occurred. Along with the introduction of firearms by the Portuguese, the end of the Warring-States Period (Sengoku Jidai) brought about a significant change in sword design. The Tokugawa government issued an edict that legislated the length and use of swords. Sword blades were made shorter, and the deep curvature of the *tachi* was straightened. The new sword was referred to as the *katana*. A new fashion of wearing the sword consisted of thrusting it through the *obi* with the cutting edge facing upward. Drawing the sword in the manner of a tachi, which consisted of wearing it with the edge turned downward as it hung from the side of the body, was no longer practical. Banno and his contemporaries faced a new challenge to Hayashizaki's method so a need for improvement and modifications for drawing the sword became essential. It was eventually Banno's student, Hasegawa Eishin, who would address the issue and create the change necessary.

SEVENTH GENERATION:
HASEGAWA CHIKARANOSUKE HIDENOBU (EISHIN), (B. LATE 1500S)

Hasegawa Chikaranosuke Hidenobu became the seventh-generation headmaster of Hayashizaki shinmei muso-ryu in 1610. Eishin, as he would come to be known, may have influenced the style more than any other man.

Eishin was born in Tosa Han (Kochi prefecture) and later moved to Edo (Tokyo) to seek employment. He was employed by the *daimyo* of Oshu as a tax collector and received an annual stipend of 1000 koku of rice. There is unfortunately no precise information about how Eishin spent his childhood and youth or the nature of his possible education in the field of martial arts. However, he is believed to have possibly been a headmaster of the *Jikiden-ryu*. This ryu was reportedly conceived in 1250 by the monk Onkeibo Chochen, who founded the style through divine inspiration. It is unknown when the school was created because there are a number of ambiguities that complicate its history, and unfortunately, Jikiden-ryu no longer exists today. The knowledge of its curriculum is based entirely on fragmentary and often unreliable information. However, there is no doubt that Eishin was influenced by the older sword school.

During Eishin's lifetime, Hayashizaki's method of drawing a tachi could no longer accommodate the Tosa samurai. The geometry and fashion of wearing a katana were far too dissimilar to that of the tachi for it to be suitable for quickly drawing and cutting. In the new position, the *saya* no longer hung loosely from the left side but instead was secured snugly against the body. This position eliminated much of the saya's freedom of movement. The *tsuka gashira* now pointed forward from the right hip with the cutting edge facing upward. It required that the swordsman grasp the sword from below the handle rather than from above as in Hayashizaki's method. These new swords were approximately two-thirds the length of their predecessor but in many ways much harder to draw. Various angles and styles of wearing them eventually came to reflect the individuality of each clan or the sword tradition they studied. Eishin devised a method of reforming the older techniques to address the change.

Eishin modified how a samurai wore the saya and tsuka gashira by having them point diagonally forward across the swordsman's body. From this position, the right and left hand had equal distance to the handle, shortening the time it took to begin the draw. This arrangement also protected the right wrist from attack while the samurai drew and placed the tsuka gashira in a situation to pressure the enemy's centerline. To accommodate the changed angle of the blade, Eishin adopted specific methods of moving into and away from the enemy while drawing. These new adaptations became known as the *Eishin-ryu* method of battojutsu. He incorporated these drawing methods and developed a set of *waza* done from *tatehiza* (half-seated posture). His methods and innovations of drawing the sword have survived to the present day.

Later in his life, Eishin returned to Tosa Han and continued to teach his form of Hayashizaki shinmei muso-ryu. His students referred to Eishin's style by several names: *Muso jikiden hidenobu-ryu, Hasegawa eishin-ryu,* Eishin-ryu, *Jikiden eishin-ryu, Hasegawa-ryu* and *Hidenobu-ryu.* The teaching of Eishin-ryu is supposed to have became widespread in Tosa Han where he was born. Regardless of whether this is true or not, his method of drawing the sword was an extremely important part of training the warriors of Tosa. Eishin's influence on their sword skills contributed greatly to the creation of new policies in their country.

Eishin and the previous six headmasters of the style lived concurrently. Most of them trained with Hayashizaki at some point during their development and either directly or as subordinates of their teachers. These headmasters were influenced by the teaching of Hayashizaki and practiced various methods of swordsmanship in addition to the techniques of Hayashizaki shinmei muso-ryu. Each of these men collectively contributed to the development of the style.

After the death of Eishin, the ryu can be traced linearly through the next thirteen generations. The tradition of awarding *menkyo kaiden* remained the same throughout history. That is to say that each man that received the *kongen no kan* (scroll of transmission) was granted the authority to carry on the style's tradition, conduct teaching and award credentials to their students. During its inception, Hayashizaki shinmei muso-ryu was never a family-inherited or owned system, as some may suggest. It is accidental that at a later time in its development, a single family passed along the traditions for several generations as a matter of political convenience.

EIGHTH GENERATION:
ARAI SEITETSU KIYONOBU, (B. EARLY 1600S)

Arai Seitetsu Kiyonobu was the eighth-generation headmaster of the ryu. He taught in Edo (Tokyo) after the departure of Eishin. He was thought to be a *ronin,* which is a masterless samurai. Considered a bit unkempt, he nevertheless attracted students that were interested in Hayashizaki shinmei muso-ryu or Eishin-ryu as it was becoming to be known as. He is credited as having taught the samurai Omori Rokuzaemon after Omori was allowed to return to the Eishin-ryu following his expulsion by Eishin. The reasons for his expulsion remain a mystery.

Omori had been a student of Eishin and was at one time the ninth headmaster of the ryu's senior while he studied with Eishin. Omori continued his study of sword techniques with the *Yagyu shinkage-ryu* of Bishu. As a student of the *Ogasawara-ryu* etiquette, Omori was greatly influenced by courtly manners, especially those found in tea ceremony. In fact, this codified set of etiquette *(ogasawara reiho)* became standardized code for all of the other traditional Japanese arts. Omori joined these codified rituals with the *saya no uchi batto gohan* (five sword-drawing forms) of the Yagyu shinkage-ryu. Omori eventually developed 11 forms of sword-drawing techniques that started from a seated posture. He considered them an improvement for teaching etiquette and swordsmanship to samurai warriors. This was because before Omori's inclusion of the ogasawara reiho, the samurai were usually educated in court etiquette and manners by studying other artistic pursuits such as the *cha no yu* (tea ceremony). With the inclusion of this education within the sword waza, the samurai acquired an education in both fencing and gentlemanly conduct.

Ninth Generation:
Hayashi Rokudayu Morimasa, (1661-1732)

Hayashi Rokudayu Morimasa was an important man of high rank who served the Tosa daimyo. Tosa samurai were stationed in the capital city of Edo and carried out various roles in the administration and affairs of state. As the Tosa daimyo's quartermaster, Hayashi had a high-ranking position, and part of his duties included serving as a cook and packhorse driver for the daimyo himself.

During this time, Hayashi studied under the watchful eye of the seventh and eighth headmasters of the Hayashizaki shinmei muso-ryu. His sword studies were varied as he also took instruction in the *Shinkage itto-ryu* and *Shinkage-ryu.* He eventually succeeded Arai as the leader of the Eishin-ryu. He consulted with and took instruction under Omori.

Omori introduced his set of forms to Hayashi. Hayashi incorporated the practice of ritualized courtesy into the training of the Hayashizaki shinmei muso-ryu and the Eishin-ryu. This development was quite possibly the turning point in the evolution of battojutsu from just a means of drawing the sword as a killing technique to what would eventually include aspects of a more philosophical pursuit. Hayashi called these forms the *omori-ryu seiza no bu.* Hayashi is officially credited with introducing the Omori-ryu to the battojutsu practitioners of Tosa Han. Later when he returned to Tosa, these forms of practice, along with the Hayashizaki shinmei muso-ryu and Eishin-ryu, were incorporated into what was then known as *Tosa iai.* They would continue to be practiced as an adjunct set of Tosa iai techniques until the 17th headmaster incorporated them as a permanent part of the Eishin-ryu curriculum.

Hayashi wrote the first official historical record of the genealogy of the ryu. It was titled the *Hiden Sho,* which translates as "secret book." His teaching methods were passed on by his family line for three generations.

10th Generation:
Hayashi Yasudayu Seisho, (d. 1776)

As high-ranking retainers of the Tosa region, the Hayashi family was very influential in the political struggles of the day. They dealt with the financial and commercial institutions within the prefecture, and their network of contacts was broad. Their children married well, and the family adopted sons to ensure their legacies. Hayashi Yasudayu Seisho was born into a samurai family that served the Tosa daimyo. He was the second son of Dogen Yasuda, a doctor of medicine in Tosa Han. Yasudayu was adopted by Hayashi and became the legal successor to his estate. He was also the second member of the Hayashi family to receive instruction as a student from Omori. Yasudayu's students were quite famous in their own right and taught Tosa iai throughout the prefecture. Yasudayu's responsibility for the ryu was passed on to his son-in-law Oguro Motoemon Kiyokatsu, who became the next headmaster.

11TH GENERATION:
OGURO MOTOEMON KIYOKATSU, (D. 1790)

Oguro was a student of 10th headmaster. Old civil documents state that Oguro's estate received 250 koku of rice per year. He became a headmaster of the ryu in 1742. Oguro was the third generation of Eishin-ryu leaders to receive instruction from Omori, although Omori must have been quite old by this time. Omori's influence over the headmasters of the Tosa iai is undisputed. As retainers of the Tokugawa Shogunate, the Hayashi samurai were bound by their duty to occasionally present themselves at court in Edo and at the emperor's court in Kyoto. The court etiquette provided by the Omori-ryu taught the necessary refinement and courtesy to the Tosa warriors.

At the turn of the 16th century, Japan was unified by Tokugawa Ieyasu. Tosa Han was politically torn apart when the victorious Tokugawa regime disassembled the Tosa forces that had opposed him. He replaced the ruling samurai of Tosa with those who had supported him during his campaign. Many of the disenfranchised samurai that had fought for the daimyo of Tosa against Tokugawa were forced to become *goshi*, which are country samurai. This does not mean that the goshi were necessarily poor. Some maintained much of their family's wealth and influence even after they had been reassigned. Both the Tosa goshi and the urban samurai continued to practice the Eishin-ryu methods of swordsmanship. However, an urban samurai had greater status and was legally able to cut down a goshi if he were to impugn his honor. Because the goshi death would be over honor, it was not socially viewed as a murder or even a crime. Privileges such as this caused a schism that led to political tensions between the two groups.

Oguro's death brought about a fracture in loyalties between the Tosa goshi and their urban cousins over who should lead the ryu. Soon after Oguro's death, a faction of the ryu was led by Matsuyoshi Hisanari, a man who was often considered more "urban" than some of his colleagues. He was a contemporary of his teacher Oguro, and because of his age, he did not lead this branch for long. He died shortly after the death of Oguro. He was succeeded by Yamakawa Kyuzo Yukikatsu (12th generation) and then Shimomura Moichi Sadamasa (13th generation) after whom this divided branch was eventually named the *Shimomura-ha eishin-ryu.*

The goshi faction was eventually led by the grandson of Hayashi's eldest son. They adopted many sons. He was named the head of this line nine years after the death of Oguro. This faction eventually became known as the *Tanimura-ha eishin-ryu,* named after the 15th headmaster. It is important to note that both branches of Tosa iai, although somewhat revamped, have continued to be taught side by side in Tosa right up to the present day.

12TH GENERATION:
HAYASHI MASU NO JO MASANARI, (D. 1818)

Hayashi Masu no Jo Masanari became the 12th-generation headmaster of Eishin-ryu of the Tanimura-ha. As previously mentioned, this development took place roughly nine years after the 11th headmaster passed away. The ryu was in turmoil as many Tosa samurai did not agree on which of Oguro's students should be recognized as his legitimate successor. This disagreement led to the two separate schools of Tosa iai being taught: the Tanimura-ha and the Shimomura-ha lines.

13TH GENERATION:
YORITA (YODA) MANZO YORIKATSU, (D. 1809)

Yorita Manzo Yorikatsu was the 13th-generation headmaster and little is known of his history. Even the date of his death is disputed. It is known that he came from a poor family and perhaps was one of the goshi (country samurai).

14TH GENERATION:
HAYASHI YADAYU SEIKI MASAYORI (MATSUTAKA), (D. 1823)

The 14th headmaster was once again a member of the Hayashi family. Hayashi Yadayu Seiki Masayori succeeded Yorita. There has been speculation that he also studied with members of the Shimomura-ha branch. The two schools were taught together in the Chidokan *dojo* in Tosa where Yadayu eventually taught.

15TH GENERATION:
TANIMURA KAME NO JO YORIKATSU, (D. 1862)

Tanimura Kame no Jo Yorikatsu taught horse riding *(bajutsu)* at the Chidokan dojo of Yadayu, the 14th headmaster. His influence was unique in that he also trained many of the aristocratic members of the Tosa samurai, which meant he undoubtedly had close contact with members of the Shimamura-ha. He taught at both the Chidokan dojo and the prefectural hall in Tosa where many of the local dignitaries studied. Tanimura was recruited to teach the Tosa iai to the Yamanouchi daimyo of Tosa. He awarded the menkyo kaiden to Yamanouchi Yodo, Kasume Hanji and Goto Magobei Seisuke, who would become the next headmaster of the Tanimura-ha line.

16TH GENERATION:
GOTO MAGOBEI MASASUKE, (D. 1898)

Goto was the headmaster of the ryu during the Meiji Restoration. His students served the emperor as fighting members of the Tosa forces during the tumultuous 1867 period. They took part in a coup staged by the feudal lords of Tosa, Choshu and Satsuma to wrest power away from the Tokugawa Shogunate and restore power to the emperor in Kyoto. Following this successful maneuver, the Tosa provincial samurai leader, Itagaki Taisuke, joined forces with Yamagata Aritomo of Choshu and Okuma Shigenobu of Hizen as administrators in reorganizing and rebuilding the Meiji government. These men were advocates of a national education system. They abhorred the narrow educational doctrines of learning by intuition that grew out of the Tokugawa Shogunate's 200-year rule of the land. As a high-ranking samurai teacher, Goto was swept up in the political charge of the day, and with the help of his successor, he began the process of making significant changes in the way Eishin-ryu's curriculum would be codified and taught.

Photo taken at Honbu dojo in Neyagawa-shi, Japan in 2000 by Carl E. Long.

Oe Masamichi Shikei

17TH GENERATION:
OE MASAMICHI SHIKEI, (1852–1927)

One of the most important headmasters of the Eishin-ryu in Tosa was Oe Masamichi Shikei. Born in Tosa in 1852, Oe, studied *Kokuri-ryu* and Shinkage-ryu kenjutsu in his youth along with Shimomura-ha eishin-ryu. He was born samurai, and when he was 15 years old, he took part in the four-day battle of Toba-Fushimi to help end the Tokugawa Shogunate forever. After the restoration of power to the emperor, he returned to Tosa and began his study of Tanimura-ha eishin-ryu under Goto.

Oe observed the time of the Meiji Restoration while the *haitorei* (the ban on wearing swords) was implemented. This edict created a painful obstacle to the continuation of kenjutsu practices. The Meiji government requested his assistance in establishing a Dai Nippon Butoku Kai school branch in Kochi prefecture because Oe was an accomplished *kendo* practitioner and teacher. He also was the recognized authority on Tosa iai. To further his education, he studied other martial arts such as *bojutsu* (stick fighting) under Itagaki Taisuke. Oe received the menkyo kaiden from both the Tanimura-ha and the Shimomura-ha teachers of Eishin-ryu. Some documents list him as having been a 15th-generation headmaster of the Shimomura-ha. However, there were other menkyo kaiden holders that also claimed the same appellation, and as a consequence, Oe renounced his position as the 15th-generation headmaster of the Shimomura-ha. Rather than fuel the controversy over leadership of either group, he combined the teaching methods of the two lines he had received from Goto and Shimomura Moichi, his two direct teachers, and renamed the style *Muso jikiden eishin-ryu.* It was Oe Masamichi that first referred to the two separate lines as the Tanimura-ha and the Shimomura-ha. Before Oe, they were both simply referred to as *Tosa eishin-ryu* with both branches claiming to be solely responsible for teaching the "orthodox method." His name designation of the two branches has survived to the present day.

Oe was recognized as an educator and reformer. He taught kendo at several local middle schools as well as the Chidokan dojo in Tosa. In 1900, he began teaching kendo and Eishin-ryu at the Kochi branch of the Dai Nippon Butoku Kai and other various local prefectural schools. In 1924, he became the second person after Nakayama Hakudo to be awarded the rank of *hanshi* in *iaido* at the Dai Nippon Butoku Kai. At the suggestion of the ministry of education and the Meiji government, Oe rearranged the Eishin-ryu curriculum to preserve its traditions and disseminate it to a wider audience. This restructuring entailed categorizing the waza of Tosa eishin-ryu by the *heiho* (strategy) that each represented and then reduce the number of waza to a more manageable number. He reorganized them into *shoden,* which was represented by the waza of the Omori-ryu; *chuden,* which reflected in the Hasegawa eishin-ryu kneeling techniques; and *okuden,* which were assigned the Hayashizaki shinmei muso-ryu standing techniques. The original *kumitachi* sets were maintained but with the addition of a set created by Oe. The new practice included a method of performing all of the tatehiza as a single form known as *hayanuki.* Oe also added the *bangai no bu,* which are a set of waza outside of the curriculum. Although, he retained many of the original techniques, he changed the names of some of the waza to aid in their understanding.

His many students went on to spread Muso jikiden eishin-ryu beyond Tosa and throughout Japan. Oe taught throughout Kochi prefecture but he also traveled extensively, giving instruction in Osaka and Kyoto. Great innovations were made in training methods at this time. He educated many excellent swordsmen; many of whom had their own ideas about the techniques. Some developed their own *kae waza* (alternatives) and shaped their own styles.

Oe died in 1927. Several of his students carried on the Muso jikiden eishin-ryu tradition. After his death, it was questioned who should become the next headmaster because Oe had left no clear designation of who would succeed him. This dispute led to much confusion and variation in the practice of the Muso jikiden eishin-ryu with several branches being formed as a consequence.

OE-MON-KA

From the very beginning, the transmission of Hayashizaki's battojutsu has used a system of indiscriminate transmission, allowing anyone in possession of full transmission to award licenses to any number of his students. Therefore, it is possible that there were multiple but unlisted holders of the menkyo kaiden in any generation. Due also in part to Oe's more open and inclusive approach to teaching Eishin-ryu, the lineages of groups currently practicing the art are fairly diverse and complex.

Oe must have believed that it was very important to make changes in the teaching curriculum in order to preserve the core values and teachings of Eishin-ryu for future generations. The samurai were no longer extant, and he chose to open up the study of Eishin-ryu for future generations. He taught many students, and through his teachings, some of his students became very accomplished and respected *iaidoka*. These students are sometimes known or referred to in Japan as *Oe-mon-ka,* meaning "under the family of Oe," as a way of showing that these accomplished students were considered as part of Oe's school lineage. From these accomplished and talented students of Oe, several have been recognized as *ju-hachi-dai,* or 18th-generation masters of Oe's ryu by various Japanese *budo* federations. For example, the designation of 18th-generation "master" denotes that these individuals were recognized and respected by their reputation and ability to carry on the Eishin-ryu tradition. This is how the continuation of Muso jikiden eishin-ryu is being carried forward through several direct current lines. Of Oe's most influential students, 16 received the kongen no kan (scroll of transmission). Some of these students were also presented with menkyo kaiden teaching licenses, although the exact number Oe awarded is unknown. One continuation of Oe's tradition, as recognized by the Dai Nippon Butoku Kai, is that of his student, Masaoka Kazumi, to his student, Narise Sakahiro, and currently to Miura Takeyuki Hidefusa.

Photo taken at Hombu dojo in Neyagawa-shi, Japan in 2000 by Carl E. Long.

Masaoka Kazumi

18TH GENERATION:
MASAOKA KAZUMI, (1896–1973)

Masaoka Kazumi was born in Kochi prefecture in 1896. His father was quite determined that his son would become a medical doctor. To make this opportunity available, Masaoka's father moved to San Francisco for work so that he would be able to support his family's financial needs in Kochi. In preparation for becoming a doctor, Masaoka received a good education.

When Masaoka reached middle school, his life took a turn in a direction that no one could have imagined. He was attending the Kochi-Ichu, one of two middle schools available to a young man of Masaoka's status. His dormitory roommate was a slightly older teenager named Mori Shigeki. Mori was Masaoka's senior and he attended the Kochi-Nichu, a second middle school situated in a separate complex. Though the two boys shared the same dormitory, they were educated at detached facilities in Kochi. For extracurricular activities, both boys studied kendo after regular classes at their respective schools. However, they shared the walk to school, carrying their kendo gear and exchanging stories. It wasn't long before Masaoka inquired about the *nihonto* (real sword) that his friend and senior always seemed to carry with him on his way to practice. Mori explained how his kendo teacher at the Kochi-Nichu instructed the students on the methods of Tosa iai. Being curious, Masaoka pleaded with him to demonstrate what he had learned, and Mori happily complied.

No one had been teaching Tosa iai at the Kochi-Ichu school. So from that day forward, Masaoka committed to memory anything he saw Mori practicing, especially drawing techniques. The Kochi-Nichu was eventually closed, and both schools ultimately combined into one. Mori's kendo teacher, Oe, was asked to remain on as the instructor at the joint school. At this point in history, it was years after the Meiji Restoration, and Oe had since restructured the Muso jikiden eishin-ryu curriculum.

Masaoka studied kendo diligently under Oe for several months. When an opportunity finally presented itself, Masaoka requested to be allowed to study with the battojutsu students that met each day after kendo classes had dispersed. At the introductory class, the great teacher of Tosa iai performed a single waza for Masaoka and requested that he attempt to replicate his movements. Masaoka reenacted what he could remember from having watched Mori. Oe was astonished by what he saw. Mori's technique was immediately recognizable, and Oe promptly accepted Masaoka as his personal student. Four additional years at Kochi-Ichu were accompanied by instruction in Oe's battojutsu. However, training only at school did not satisfy Masaoka's hunger for more instruction in the ryu. He began to supplement his training by attending classes that Oe taught at the Kochi prefecture Butoku Kai. Members of the dojo included Nakanishi Iwaki and Takemura Shinzuo, two of the most senior members of the ryu. According to Masaoka's accounts, many in Tosa concluded at the time that Nakanishi would one day be Oe's successor.

Masaoka acquired quite a reputation as a skilled *kendoka*. When the Dai Nihon Butoku Kai established a new direction for the Budo Senmon Gakko at the Butokuden, Oe requested that Masaoka move to Kyoto to attend and teach kendo at the great hall. In 1917, at the age of 21, he left Kochi and moved to Kyoto. The school was attended by those who had received high scholastic scores and showed great promise as instructors of budo. At the school, they studied Japanese archery, *naginata* and *kambun* (Chinese writing). During the breaks and holidays, Masaoka continued to make frequent trips to train with his teacher in Kochi. When Masaoka graduated from it, he was asked to stay, teach kendo and participate in the *kenkyusei*, which is advanced research and training. In 1919, during the first year of kenkyusei, Masaoka's teacher, Oe, was finally invited to demonstrate Tosa iai.

The sword arts program at the Butokuden had included kendo *kata* but iaijutsu was not taught. Oe's performance of Tosa iai stirred the audience that day, and many of the students prodded Masaoka to teach them what they had seen. It was a proud day for Oe's student because he watched his teacher demonstrate Tosa iai before a panel of dignitaries and administrators of the Taisho government.

Two years after Oe's visit to the Butokuden, Masaoka was awarded the *renshi shogo* title in the arts of kendo and iaido by the Dai Nihon Butoku Kai. He was subsequently transferred to the city of Kanazawa to work as a teacher. He also transferred his Butoku Kai membership to the local branch in Ishikawa prefecture. His duties there as a middle school teacher and budo instructor highlighted his positive qualities as a high-caliber man. His kendo team won the Japan national championship. Then in 1924, when Oe was awarded the *hanshi* title—the highest level of attainment issued by the Dai Nihon Butoku Kai—Masaoka received the menkyo kaiden from his teacher to be able to pass on Muso jikiden eishin-ryu. After two more years, Oe bestowed on Masaoka the kongen no kan, which represented the complete transmission of the Tosa iai. Masaoka's reputation quickly spread, and in Kanazawa, the news reached another famous teacher of budo. The membership of the Ishikawa branch of the Butoku Kai also included the swordsman Nakayama Hakudo. When news arrived that a second Tosa iai teacher, particularly one who had received the highest transmission from Oe, reached Hakudo, he was astonished. Nakayama Hakudo had also trained with Oe in Tosa, but he never received a menkyo kaiden from him. Nakayama's menkyo kaiden certification had come from within the Shimomura-ha.

Kanazawa was a small city, and as such, the two accomplished swordsmen developed a great friendship. Nakayama formally expressed his gratitude to the Budo Senmon Gakko for having sent Masaoka to teach and share his knowledge. The kendo taught in Kanazawa became well-respected because of the teaching efforts of both Masaoka and Nakayama.

Oe died in 1927, and in the year of his teacher's death, the Butoku Kai granted Masaoka the *kyoshi shogo* in iaido. Very few men with the kyoshi title in iaido existed at this time, and Masaoka was humbled to be one of the first recognized. It was at this time that Masaoka gained respect for Nakayama's knowledge of the Shimomura-ha. The two discussed many aspects of Tosa iai, and Masaoka looked up to his senior while he examined and learned Nakayama's approach to swordsmanship. Nakayama had been changing his approach to Tosa iai. as well. New political developments and Japan's national war efforts were ramping up. The relationship between the two men and their notoriety within the new administration did not sit well with some members of the old Chidokan dojo in Tosa. Other menkyo kaiden holders quickly responded to Oe's death with their own claims of succession. The ministry of education and the Dai Nihon Butoku Kai set about recognizing all of their combined efforts in an attempt to unify the koryu schools under an umbrella of Japanese national spirit and maintain its old traditions.

BATTOJUTSU IN MODERN JAPAN

The world would witness two-and-a-half decades of war and suffering in which the Japanese military machine would play a major role. The Japanese military recruited Nakayama, Sasaburo Takano and others to create a set of kata and test-cutting drills for their recruits at the Toyama military academy in Tokyo.

These sets were an amalgamation of koryu and kendo exercises constructed to resemble standing versions of the older kenjutsu movements. Their purpose was to prepare Japanese soldiers for wielding the katana in close-quarters combat. Fourteen years later, other members of the Tosa iai schools were called on to assist the Butoku Kai in creating sword-training methods that were taught to young military cadets as they prepared for war in the South Pacific.

In 1939, menkyo kaiden holders from Tosa were encouraged to institute a set of battojutsu techniques that could be taught to naval officers. Fukui Harumasa and Kono Hyakuren, who were Oe-mon-ka students from Tosa, assembled a set of 10 techniques based on older Tosa iai waza. This set of waza became known as the *dai nihon batto-ho waza* (sword-drawing methods of Greater Japan). Later some of the menkyo kaiden holders formed an independent organization based in Osaka for master-level Oe-mon-ka. It was named the Dai Nihon Yaegaki-Kai and supported efforts to widely disseminate Oe's teachings. They established branch dojo throughout the Kansai region, some of which continue to thrive even today.

After the fall of the Japanese forces at the end of World War II, the Supreme Commander of Allied Powers (SCAP) directed all Japanese organizations that appeared to be military-related to be dissolved. The Dai Nihon Butoku Kai voluntarily surrendered their charter and disbanded. The citizens of Japan were forced to reevaluate the role traditional *bujutsu* played in their development since the Meiji Restoration. The SCAP directives were finally lifted in 1952.

After the surrender of Japan, Masaoka returned to Shikoku to became a farmer for a number of years. He returned to the battojutsu community after the SCAP ban on budo was lifted. He then returned to Kanazawa to teach again. Shortly thereafter, sword studies were no longer banned, and practice resumed in Japan. In the same year that the SCAP directives were lifted, the Zen Nihon Kendo Renmei (All Japan Kendo Federation) was established. Two of the first members were Nakayama and Masaoka. In 1953, the Dai Nippon Butoku Kai was also reestablished with a new charter and new philosophical mission.

Several other organizations began to form, and in 1954, the Zen Nippon Iaido Renmei organized and appointed Kono Hyakuren as the general director. The Zen Nippon Iaido Renmei sponsored the first iaido tournament in 1955 with demonstrations and performances by Fukui and Nakayama.

One year later, the All Japan Kendo Federation added an iaido division to the organization. Masaoka was appointed the director. The federation promoted Masaoka to the rank of seventh *dan* in kendo and awarded him the first iaido eighth-dan hanshi in 1957. This was followed by his being awarded the ninth dan five years later in 1962 when he turned 66 years of age. Throughout his directorship, Masaoka was adamant about maintaining the traditional methods of swordsmanship. As a director of the iaido branch of the Kendo Renmei, he was concerned over the changes that were taking place within the iaido methods of the kendo practitioners. The movements were evolving into waza that resembled the kata of kendo. These were quite unlike the koryu techniques. At the urging of the board of directors, a panel was formed in 1967 to create a standardized set of iaido kata based on the older sword methods. Masaoka was selected as the Muso jikiden eishin-ryu representative in the creation of these forms.

As a menkyo kaiden of the ryu, he was committed to preserving its traditions and combat-effective strategy. He wrote two manuals that described the methods and practices he had learned from Oe. His first was titled *Muso Jikiden Eishin-Ryu Ten no Maki,* and it describes the fundamentals of Tosa iai and the 11 shoden waza of the Omori-ryu. The second manual, *Eishin-Ryu Iai Heiho Chi no Maki,* describes the entire curriculum of Tosa iai as he had learned it from Oe Masamichi. It was Masaoka's belief that that master-level swordsmen should be able to recognize fundamental principles and concepts common to all good sword methods. He formulated judging criteria for iaido based on the principles described in Chapter 4 of this book. Although Masaoka never fulfilled his father wishes to become a doctor, he was committed to his father's ideals. Both of Masaoka's children became doctors at his urging. In 1973, Masaoka finished teaching a children's kendo class near his home in Kanazawa. He removed his headgear and, while still dressed in his *bogu,* passed away at the age 77.

THE VISION FOR THE FUTURE

Post-war Japan brought about the revitalization of many of the ancient martial arts. With the reestablishment of the Dai Nippon Butoku Kai, Zen Nihon Kendo Renmei and the Zen Nihon Iaido Renmei, the traditional martial arts of Japan were reintroduced to the general public as a means of instilling a new Japanese spirit. The newly formed organizations brought together the headmasters of many ancient ryu to establish a new direction for the ancient martial traditions. The mission of the reestablished organizations was to maintain the ancient art forms while stressing the *"do"* (the pursuit of self-actualization) attained through the practice of Japanese sword arts. The iaido seeds that had been planted centuries before had finally found fertile ground from which to grow and blossom. Battojutsu became an art form devoted to the improvement of society as a whole through the development of the individual. This quest for self-improvement became the primary focus of most of the post-war martial traditions. The essence of the teachings began to focus on budo rather than bujutsu during the latter half of the 20th century.

Hayashizaki's sword methods had endured many controversial events throughout the centuries. The ryu had split into several factions, and each espoused its own etymology. The lineage of the Eishin-ryu was not without its controversy, and by the 1950s, several practitioners were hailed as the rightful heir to the mantle of *soshi* (overall headmaster). These claims aside, all of the teachers of the Eishin-ryu school of swordsmanship espoused the practice of battojutsu as a form of self-development in addition to the strategic and tactical lessons it offered. By following the examples of these great men, practitioners of today inherit the wisdom, compassion and technical expertise to carry their vision forward as stewards for the next generation of men and women.

TOSA EISHIN-RYU IAI AND AUTHORS' GENEALOGY

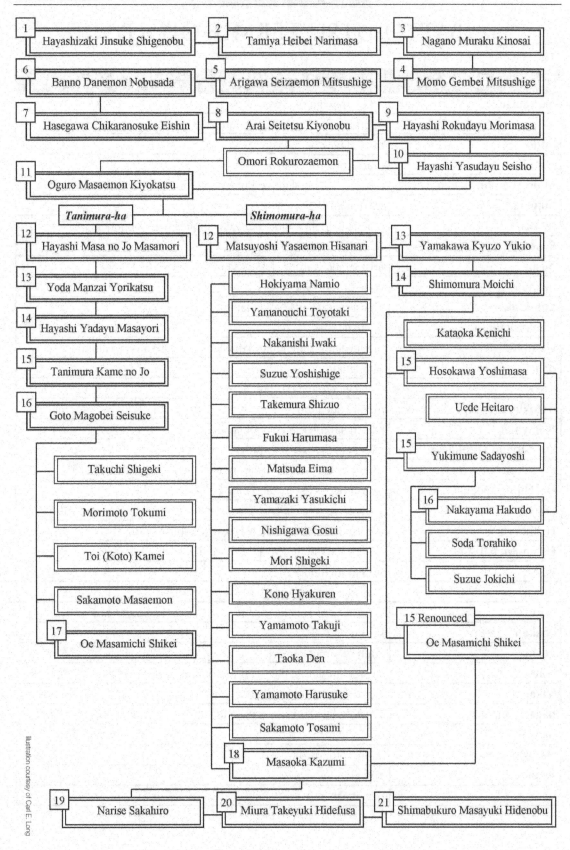

Illustration courtesy of Carl E. Long

1 Hayashizaki Jinsuke Shigenobu
2 Tamiya Heibei Narimasa
3 Nagano Muraku Kinosai
6 Banno Danemon Nobusada
5 Arigawa Seizaemon Mitsushige
4 Momo Gembei Mitsushige
7 Hasegawa Chikaranosuke Eishin
8 Arai Seitetsu Kiyonobu
9 Hayashi Rokudayu Morimasa
Omori Rokurozaemon
10 Hayashi Yasudayu Seisho
11 Oguro Masaemon Kiyokatsu

Tanimura-ha

Shimomura-ha

12 Hayashi Masa no Jo Masamori
12 Matsuyoshi Yasaemon Hisanari
13 Yamakawa Kyuzo Yukio
13 Yoda Manzai Yorikatsu
Hokiyama Namio
14 Shimomura Moichi
14 Hayashi Yadayu Masayori
Yamanouchi Toyotaki
Kataoka Kenichi
15 Tanimura Kame no Jo
Nakanishi Iwaki
15 Hosokawa Yoshimasa
16 Goto Magobei Seisuke
Suzue Yoshishige
Uede Heitaro
Takemura Shizuo
Takuchi Shigeki
Fukui Harumasa
15 Yukimune Sadayoshi
Morimoto Tokumi
Matsuda Eima
16 Nakayama Hakudo
Toi (Koto) Kamei
Yamazaki Yasukichi
Soda Torahiko
Nishigawa Gosui
Sakamoto Masaemon
Mori Shigeki
Suzue Jokichi
17 Oe Masamichi Shikei
Kono Hyakuren
Yamamoto Takuji
15 Renounced
Taoka Den
Oe Masamichi Shikei
Yamamoto Harusuke
Sakamoto Tosami
18 Masaoka Kazumi
19 Narise Sakahiro
20 Miura Takeyuki Hidefusa
21 Shimabukuro Masayuki Hidenobu

APPENDIX C
BATTOJUTSU TERMINOLOGY

General Terms	
battojutsu	art of drawing the sword
bogu	*kendo* armor or protective equipment
budo	martial way
budoka	practitioner of *budo*
Budo Senmon Gakko	martial art school at the Butokuden for training *budo* instructors
bujutsu	martial art
bunkai	practical application of *kata* techniques (with opponent)
Busen	Budo Senmon Gakko
bushi	aristocratic warrior class of samurai
bushido	code of warrior ethics
Butokuden	oldest martial arts hall in Japan
Chokuden-ryu	*naginata* style
chuden	midlevel transmission of knowledge (in *koryu* curriculum)
dan	step, grade
dojo	place where *budo* is practiced
dotoku	moral education
daimyo	provincial ruler in ancient Japan
Dai Nippon Butoku Kai	Great Japan Martial Virtues Association
dai nihon batto-ho	sword set created by Eishin-ryu teachers for naval officers
Dai Nihon Yaegaki Kai	Osaka-based organization for *Eishin-ryu* masters
Edo	ancient name of Tokyo, also a period in Japan, A.D. 1603-1867
Eishin-ryu	iaijutsu style created by Hasegawa Eishin
Eishin-ryu batto-ho	set of 11 standing *waza* for the Dai Nihon Butoku Kai
embu	display, demonstration
fukyu	to disseminate information
gakusei	student
gekken	kendo
goshi	country samurai
haitorei	sword ban during the Meiji Restoration
hakama	wide pleated trousers
hakama sabaki	spreading the hakama legs to the left and right with the right hand
hanshi	final *shogo* title, model teacher, equivalent of *menkyo kaiden*
Hayashi Myojin	*kami*, spirit of Hayashizaki shrine
haori	outer kimono jacket
hera	peg attached to *koshita* inside rear of *hakama*

Hiden Sho	book written by Hayashi Rokudayu, the ninth-generation master of *Eishin-ryu*
himo	cord, lace
iaido	way of being in the moment with the sword
iaijutsu	art of being in the moment with the sword
Jikiden-ryu	a sword style created by Onkeibo Chochu in A.D. 1250
jo	castle
joseki	upper side
joza	upper seat
juban	undergarment
kabuto	helmet
kaicho	association president
kaku obi	square kimono belt
kamae	posture and attitude
kami	spirit or diety
kamidana	spirit shelf
kami no ashi	foot closest to *kamiza*
kamiza	highest place of honor, seat of the *kami*
kambun	study of Chinese writing system
kancho	head of the house or building
kanji	training
keikogi	training jacket
kendo	way of the sword
kendo no kata	standardized *kata* for *kendo*
kenjutsu	art of sword fighting (with partner)
kenkyu	research
kenkyusei	advanced study at the Budo Senmon Gakko
kenshi	swordsman
kihon	basic techniques
kobudo	old martial arts
Kochi-Ichu, Kochi-Nichu	middle schools in Kochi prefecture
kohai	a student who is a junior to his classmates
koku	a bushel of rice
kongen no kan (maki)	scroll of original teachings, the highest honor in *Eishin-ryu*
koryu	traditional school started before the Meiji Restoration
koshita	board at back of *hakama*
kumitachi, katachi	sword training with partner
kyoshi	second *shogo* title, warrior instructor
kyu	beginner's ranking
matadachi	split at side of *hakama*
menkyo	license
menkyo kaiden	highest transmission and license to teach

michi	road or pathway
MJER	*Muso jikiden eishin-ryu*
mon (kamon)	family crest
montsuki	wide-sleeve top with *mon* on chest, sleeve and back
mudansha	person without *dan* ranking
Muraku-ryu	sword style developed by Nagano Muraku Kinrosai
musha shugyo	pilgrimage of austere training
Muso jikiden eishin-ryu	sword style created by Oe Masamichi
muto	no sword
obi	belt
Oe-mon-ka	direct students of Oe Masamichi
okuden	deep level of transmission of knowledge (in *koryu* curriculum)
Onno-ha itto-ryu	sword style developed by Ittosai Kagehisa
reigi	etiquette
reiho	method of expressing etiquette
renshi	first *shogo* title, accomplished warrior
renshu	hard training
ritsurei	standing bow
ronin	masterless samurai
ryu	style or tradition
saho reiho	method of preparation and etiquette
samurai	Japan's warrior class
saya no uchi batto gohon	five drawing techniques of *Shinkage-ryu*
SCAP	Supreme Commander of Allied Forces in World War II
seitei kata	standardized forms created by the Zen Nippon Kendo Renmei
seiza	to sit correctly
sempai	a person who is senior to others
Sengoku Jidai	Warring-States Period in Japan from mid-15th century to early 17th century
sensei	one who has gone before, a teacher or master
shiai	match, competition
shihan	highest ranked teacher in a *dojo,* sixth *dan* or above
Shimomura-ha	a branch style of *Eishin-ryu*
shimo no ashi	foot farthest from *kamiza*
shimoseki	low side of the *dojo,* to the left of *shomen*
shimoza	lower seat of honor, directly across from the *shomen*
shinden	spirit house
Shinkage-ryu	16th-century sword style created by Kamizumi Nobutsuna
shinsa	grading
shinsa in	chief official for grading
Shinto	animistic religion of Japan
shisei	posture

shitachi	the winning combatant of pre-planned *kumitachi*
shi-tei-ai	teacher-student relationship
shizan	cutting practice
shizentai	natural posture
shoden	first level of transmission of knowledge (in *koryu* curriculum)
shodo	Japanese brush writing
shogo	samurai titles awarded to high-ranked teachers for their character and skill
shogun	military leader of Japan
shomen	forward wall of the *dojo,* highest area
soshi, soshihan	overall master of an organization
suemonogiri	testing one's ability to cut
tabi	formal soft footwear for inside the *dojo*
tachirei	standing bow with the sword
taikai	competition, tournament
tameshigiri	test cutting
Tanimura-ha	a branch style of *Eishin-ryu*
tatami	floor covering mats made of rice straw
tori	to grab
Tosa Han	modern Kochi prefecture
tosho	sword maker
uchitachi	the losing, attacking side in pre-planned *kumitachi*
uke	to receive or block
uwagi	*iaido/kendo* training jacket
wara	cutting targets of rolled *tatami omote*
waza	technique
Yagyu shinkage-ryu	style revised by Yagyu Muneyoshi
yudansha	person with *dan* ranking
yugei	performance art
zarei	seated bow
Zen Nippon Kendo Renmei	All Japan Kendo Federation
Zen Nippon Iaido Renmei	All Japan Iaido Federation

Phrases in the Dojo

ato	back
domo arigato gozaimasu	thank you very much (very formal)
hajime	begin
katana o motte	get your swords
kiritsu	stand up
matte	wait
mawatte	turn around

mokosu	silence (meditation)
osame	end
otagai ni rei	bow to each other
rei	bow
seiretsu	stand in line
sensei ni rei	bow to the teacher
shomen ni rei	bow to the front side
to-rei	bow to the sword
yame	stop

Technical Terms and Techniques

aiuchi	strike together
ashisabaki	footwork
ate	strike
ayumi-ashi	"natural moving of foot forward," footwork when walking
bangai no bu	"outside the curriculum," *kata* set created by Oe Masamichi
batto	to draw the sword
chiburi	shaking blood from the sword
chikama-ai	short distance
chudan no kamae	middle-level guard posture
chuden	middle-level transmission
datto	remove the sword from *obi*
datsu ryoku	relaxed movement
eishaku rei	15-degree bow
enshin-ryoku	centripetal force
fumikomi	moving forward with a stamping foot
furikaburi	raising the sword to cut
gedan no kamae	lower-level guard posture
gyaku kesa-giri	diagonal upward cut
gyakute noto	reversed grip *noto*
hai-rei	bow to the environment, toward the *shomen*
hanzoroe	one foot half step behind the other
happo-giri	eight-direction cut
harai	to sweep
hasso no kamae	sword *kamae* above right shoulder
hasuji otosu	line of the cut
hayanuki	all MJER *chuden kata* performed successively without stopping
heiho	strategy
hidari jodan no kamae	left foot forward with the sword held above the head
hikitaoshi	to pull downward
iai	in the moment, drawing the sword in face-to-face combat

iaigoshi	to support the body at the hips in a lowered posture
irimi tenshin	enter and turn
jiku-ashi	foot turning on the spot on toes and heel
jodan no kamae	upper-level guard posture
kae waza	alternative form of a technique
karuma	*waki no kamae* with horizontal sword
katate	with one hand
kesa-giri	diagonal downward cut
kime	focus
kiriage	upward cut
kirigaeshi	reversal of the cutting movement
kiri-ma	cutting distance
kirioroshi	downward finishing cut
kiriotoshi	downward dropping cut
kiritsuke	a decisive cut
koiguchi no kiri gata	"cutting the carp's mouth," pushing the *tsuba* from the *saya*
kokyu	breath
koshi mawari	turning the hips
kuzushi	balance
ma	space or area
maai	combined or relative space between two objects
metsuke	focus and direction of the gaze of the eyes
migi jodan no kamae	left foot forward with the sword held above the head
moku-rei	silent bow
morote	with both hands
muto-dori	empty-hand sword taking techniques
musubiashi	feet together
nito	two swords
noto	resheathing the sword
nukitsuke	drawing and cutting with tip of sword
nukiuchi	drawing and cutting with the *monouchi*
o-chiburi	large *chiburi*
okuden	deep-level transmission of knowledge
riai	purposeful practice of principles and strategies
sei-chu-sen	the centerline of the opponent's line of combat
saya-ate	collision between the scabbards of two persons
saya banare	the position of the *kissaki* just prior to separation from the *saya*
sayabiki	pushing back the *saya*
saya no uchi	inside the *saya*
seiza no bu	*waza* that begin from the seated position
seme-ashi	pressing or pushing with the foot
semete	pressing or pushing with the hand

shibori	wringing and gripping of the hands on the *tsuka* while cutting
shinite	"dead hands"
shirei	a bow to the teacher
shisha tachi	scouting sword
shoden	first level of transmission of knowledge
soe-ashi	supporting foot
soete	supporting hand
soete tsuki	thrust with a supporting hand on the *mune*
suihei	level like water
suki	an opening in the defense, physical or mental
sunegakoi	blocking an attack to the lower leg
tachi waza	standing techniques
taisabaki	body movement
taito	wearing the sword
tate-ha	drawing with cutting edge facing upward
tatehiza	half-seated position with one knee standing
tate noto	*noto* with cutting edge facing upward
teki	enemy
te no uchi	control of hands, correct grip, timing of *shibori*
tenshin	turning off the centerline to avoid an attack
toho	sword method
toma-ai	large distances
to-rei	bow to the sword
tsubazeriai	two *tsuba* that are pressed together to find a *suki* in the enemy's defense
tsuki-ashi	thrusting step
tsuka no nigiri kata	method of gripping the *tsuka*
tsuki	thrust
uchi	strike
ukenagashi	to receive and flow
ukete	blocking hand
waki no kamae	*kamae* with sword hidden to the side and behind the body
yoko chiburi	flick *chiburi* to the right side
yokomenuchi	cut to the side of the head

Philosophical Concepts

burei	lack of etiquette
chu	loyalty
dai kyo soku kei	big, strong, fast, light
enzan no metsuke	gazing at the distant mountains
fukaku	depth of character and understanding
gi	righteousness

gijutsu	polished technique
go no sen	to attack after the initiative has been seized
heijoshin	a peaceful mind that is unaffected by the environment
homare	honor
ichi go, iche e	one encounter, one chance
ichi-nen	single-mindedness, determination
iwao no mi	immovable body like stone
jaki o dasu	mental cleansing
jikishin	a direct and pure heart and mind
jikishin kore dojo nari	the *dojo* resides within a true heart
jin	compassion
jinkaku	outgoing and personable character
jo ha kyu	modulation of timing, intention and speed
jutsu	art
katsu jin ken	life-giving sword
ken i ichi	*kenjutsu* and *iai* go together
kenkyo	modesty
kensho	moment of enlightenment
ki	energy and spiritual power
kiai	unifying and focusing the energy through technique
kigurai	attitude and dignity in demeanor
kihaku	focused intent
ki ken tai ichi	spirit, sword and body are one
kokoro	heart, mind
kokoro dashi	big dreams
kokoro no tame ni	for the next generation
kyorei	action without sincerity
makoto (shisei)	sincerity
midashi nami	one's appearance
muga	without ego
munen	without thought
mushin	an unfixed mind
muso-ken	dream sword
Nihon kokoro	Japanese spirit
on-giri	duty and obligation
rei	respect
satsu jin to	life-taking sword
saya no naka no kachi	victory while still in the *saya*
seishin	correct spirit
sen	to seize the initiative
sen no sen	to seize the initiative before the opponent

sen sen no sen	attacking between the opponent's decision to attack and his first movement
shitsurei	pure heart and intention
shu ha ri	to copy, to diverge and to transcend the teachings
sutemi	sacrifice
tachi-kaze	sword wind, the sound of the sword as it cuts through the air
tenshin sho	divine inspiration
uko muko	having and not having
yoyu	the ability to change at any moment , margin
yu	courage
zanshin	lingering awareness of the environment